TAKE CONTROL
OF YOUR WORRY

TAKE CONTROL
OF YOUR WORRY

MANAGING GENERALISED
ANXIETY DISORDER

DR LISA LAMPE

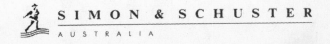

SIMON & SCHUSTER
AUSTRALIA

TAKE CONTROL OF YOUR WORRY
First published in Australia in 2004 by
Simon & Schuster (Australia) Pty Limited
Suite 2, Lower Ground Floor
14-16 Suakin Street
Pymble, NSW 2073

A Viacom Company
Sydney New York London Toronto

Visit our website at www.simonsaysaustralia.com

Cataloguing-in-Publication data:

Lampe, Lisa.
  Take control of your worry: managing generalised
  anxiety disorder.

  Bibliography.
  Includes index.
  ISBN 0 7318 1219 0.

  1. Anxiety. 2. Anxiety disorders. 3. Anxiety – Popular
  works. 4. Psychiatry – Popular works. 5. Rational-emotive
  psychotherapy. I. Title.

616.85223

Cover and internal design by Christabella Designs
Typeset in 11 on 14 Sabon by Kirby Jones
Printed in Australia by Griffin Press

10 9 8 7 6 5 4 3 2 1

To my parents.

Acknowledgments

I am grateful to all my teachers over the years—the many colleagues who generously gave their advice and shared their knowledge, and the many patients who helped me to understand this illness. Their feedback during treatment provided the impetus for my strategies to evolve.

Contents

INTRODUCTION

If you suffer from too much worry in your life; if you can't enjoy the present because you're too worried about the future; if being told to 'relax' one more time makes you want to tear your hair out … then, this book is for you.

Too much worry can engulf up to 90 per cent of your day, and make it impossible for you to ever feel relaxed. It can ruin your sleep and interfere with your life at home, at work and socially. Decision-making can seem ridiculously stressful and a tidal wave of procrastination may be waiting to overwhelm you. Add to this chronic exhaustion, headaches, irritability and constant tension and you probably have generalised anxiety disorder, 'the worry illness'. Whether you have all these symptoms (and more) or just a tendency to worry too much sometimes, this book has strategies that can help.

For more than ten years I have specialised in the assessment and treatment of anxiety problems. In that time I have seen great books appear for the general reader that deal with panic attacks, agoraphobia, obsessive compulsive disorder and social anxiety (all of which I will describe in detail later), but the worriers of the world have been sadly neglected.

There are many reasons for this. In the past, doctors didn't realise just how distressing, and even disabling, too much worry—and all the unpleasant physical symptoms that go with it—can be for the sufferer. Secondly, there wasn't much research into the problem (one of the reasons that doctors and psychologists didn't know much about it).

Thirdly, most worriers tended to suffer in silence, thinking that it was just in their nature to worry so much. So, although as therapists we could have learned a lot from sufferers by asking them about all their worry symptoms, we didn't realise how common the problem was, and we didn't know the sorts of questions to ask. Even less was known about how to treat it!

It wasn't too long ago that doctors considered anxiety disorders to be fairly minor complaints—and I say this as a doctor myself, looking back on my own training in medical school. We were very wrong! As anyone who has suffered any type of anxiety disorder will confirm, severe anxiety is distressing, demoralising, even downright depressing. It can stop you from doing the things you want to do in life, or from getting as much pleasure from life as you could. In particular, too much worry is exhausting. Most sufferers sleep poorly and feel chronically tired.

As I continued my work at a clinic specialising in research into and treatment of anxiety disorders I was privileged to be able to talk to hundreds of anxiety sufferers about their symptoms and experiences of treatment. I learned an enormous amount from them. At the same time, working in a university research environment, I was able to keep up with the very latest developments in research both from my own unit and overseas. The new information emerging about the nature of worry was very exciting. It led, in turn, to the development of new and effective treatment strategies. I became much better at recognising excessive worry, and when I tried out the new treatment strategies with my patients they worked! It was possible to help people learn how to master their worry very effectively.

As I began to work with a lot more people, I developed some handouts and worksheets to help explain things better and give my patients something they could take away with them and read at home. I began to wish there was a readily available book to describe the new treatment strategies in everyday terms. Then I thought that perhaps I should write that book. It turned out that there was a publisher who agreed. Then I just had to sit down and write it!

My principal goal in writing *Take Control of Your Worry* is to describe useful strategies for controlling excessive worry. I describe the strategies in everyday language and in enough detail to enable you to use them effectively even if you don't have the support of a therapist. They can equally well be used in conjunction with therapeutic help—some of the strategies are easier to master than others, some people have more severe or complicated anxiety than others, and there are times when it can be helpful to get assistance from a trained professional.

All the strategies in this book are skills that can be mastered. In many cases it is simply a matter of changing habits. Worry is essentially a habit that some people have developed in response to stress and uncertainty in their life. This book is basically about replacing unhelpful habits of worrying about problems and stresses with more effective new habits.

Your doctor may still not know what questions to ask, since much of our knowledge about worry is quite recent, but after reading this book you will know exactly what to tell your doctor to get any help you need.

WHO CAN BENEFIT FROM THIS BOOK

I would like to state right now that, even if you consider yourself an old dog, you *can* still learn new tricks. There is no age limit on who can benefit from the techniques described in this book. I have treated men and women in their seventies and even eighties. I have no doubt that even older individuals could benefit, but so far no one older than this has come to ask me for help. I hope that this is because worry is less of a problem at this age and not because potential sufferers feel that nothing can be done. There are many strategies that can be helpful even if you feel that you're not quite as sharp as you used to be.

The strategies in this book have also been used effectively with children and teenagers. The sense of greater control that mastering these techniques brings can be a boost to self-confidence and self-esteem at a vulnerable time of life. There is a clear structure to follow with each strategy and the instructions are down to earth, which helps the 'therapy' to feel less intimidating.

MAKING THIS BOOK WORK FOR YOU

To give yourself the best chance of gaining some benefit, I am asking you to make one commitment to yourself: *give the strategies in this book a fair trial.* As I describe the strategies I will, in most cases, give an indication of how often they need to be practised to be effective and how soon you can expect to see some benefit. You owe it to yourself to give each strategy an adequate trial of consistent practice over at least the time indicated before deciding that it doesn't help. Not all the strategies will benefit everyone, but the more strategies you try the more chance you have of finding ones that will help you. There is, alas, no wonder drug or miracle technique. The secret of success is to apply a range of strategies that all make a small contribution.

Chapter One

UNDERSTANDING ANXIETY

You know the feelings only too well: the sense of fear or dread, the physical symptoms of tension, heart palpitations, nausea, difficulty catching your breath ... These symptoms are all part of what is known as the 'flight or fight response'.

THE FLIGHT OR FIGHT RESPONSE

As far as we know, all animals have some type of flight or fight response. Its purpose is to increase the chances of survival in case of a sudden physical threat to the animal. Survival might be enhanced through flight—running away—or by fighting off the threat; for example, another animal that is attacking. The flight or fight response gives an animal extra speed and strength. It's important to fully understand this response because problems with excessive anxiety occur in humans when the flight or fight response is switched on inappropriately. Part of the treatment of anxiety is learning how to prevent this from happening.

So, how is the flight or fight response switched on and what effects does it have? There is always some trigger. In animals this is usually instinctive, although animals, like humans can also *learn* to fear things (more about this later). In the wild, there are certain signs in the environment that an animal will instinctively realise represent potential danger. For example, the scent of a predator or the smell of smoke in the air will send many animals running. In other cases the trigger may be visual—a shadow overhead will send a ground animal like a rabbit for cover—or audible—a sudden loud noise, for example. From its conception the association of certain triggers with danger is programmed into the animal. Once it becomes aware of one of these triggers, the flight or fight response is immediately and automatically triggered. This, in turn, triggers the release of a number of chemicals and hormones, among them, adrenaline.

Adrenaline is a hormone manufactured in small glands near the kidneys (the adrenal glands). When it is released into the bloodstream many of the most prominent symptoms of the flight or fight response result. Adrenaline acts directly on the heart to increase both the speed and the strength of the heartbeat. This explains why so many people report not only a rapid heartbeat but also an increased awareness of their heart beating in their chest. The reaction can be frightening when you don't realise that there is a good reason for it and that it's not a sign something is wrong with your heart. With the heart beating more strongly, blood is pumped vigorously around the body and may contribute to the flushed, hot feeling that many people experience. Adrenaline also results in increased sweating, dry mouth and dilation of the pupils. An adrenaline surge can also result in a strong urge to empty the bowels or bladder because of effects on the gastrointestinal system.

All these changes are designed to enhance an animal's capacity to run and escape. The extra blood flow goes largely to the muscles to prime them for action, the increased sweating assists with the cooling process.

At the same time as adrenaline is released, there is also a rise in cortisol levels. However, this hormone works mainly in the background and its effects are not immediately obvious. When cortisol levels are frequently or persistently elevated there may be a reduction in immunity levels. High cortisol levels have also been linked with depression and poor sleep.

Through this series of chemical releases and resulting physiological effects, a wide range of physical symptoms may be experienced:

- dizziness
- trouble thinking clearly
- difficulty concentrating
- blurred vision
- sense of unreality
- sense of being outside your own body
- headache
- dry mouth
- lump in the throat
- trouble swallowing
- feeling of constriction in the throat
- pounding heart
- chest pain or tightness
- muscle pain and tension
- trouble breathing
- 'butterflies' in the stomach
- feeling too hot
- nausea
- vomiting
- diarrhoea
- frequent urination
- shakiness
- trembling
- blushing
- sweating.

Of course, you may not experience all of these symptoms. Each person tends to have their own particular pattern.

If you were to use these physical effects to help you run faster than you ever thought possible—in order to escape your attacker or an approaching fire—you wouldn't really be aware of them. However, when you get this reaction because you are worrying about something, you're not actually going anywhere. In this situation, you will tend to be acutely aware of the physical changes in your body.

This in itself can be a cause of further worry: 'What if there is something wrong with my heart?' 'Am I going crazy?' If you've had these worries as a result of the physical symptoms of anxiety, you are not alone. It is important to stress that the acute flight or fight reaction is neither harmful nor dangerous to your body. However, it is certainly extremely unpleasant and, as noted above, it is possible that there are some long-term effects from being constantly anxious that might make you less than optimally healthy.

TRIGGERING THE FLIGHT OR FIGHT RESPONSE IN HUMANS

There are some interesting differences between human beings and animals when it comes to how the flight or fight response can be triggered. This is as a result of the much bigger brain that humans have grown.

Proportional to their size, animals generally have a smaller brain than humans. Animal brains are largely designed to control the functioning of the body: breathing, temperature control, heartbeat. There are also areas for controlling muscle activity and interpreting information from the senses.

The human brain is much larger. Like animals, we have a part of the brain that controls basic bodily functions and muscle activity. However, a lot more brain is devoted to processing sensory information. Incredible connections link different areas of the brain, so that one piece of sensory information is dealt with by many of its parts.

Human beings have also developed the capacity for abstract thought and imagination. We can consider not only what *is*, but also what *was* and what *might be* ... and this can cause problems! For example, 'That shadow ... it's probably just a tree ... but it *could* be a person ... and what if that person is about to attack me?' If we experience these kinds of thoughts, we will immediately feel rather anxious. In other words, we will have triggered the flight or fight response.

How do we do this? Well, in humans the flight or fight response is rarely triggered instinctively in a full-blown way, although there are many natural environmental phenomena that make a lot of people a bit anxious, like heights, snakes and storms. For a few people their anxiety about these things may become an actual phobia, and might trigger a strong flight or fight response.

However, in general, a human only experiences a full-blown flight or fight response once they have *decided* that a situation is threatening or dangerous. In other words, we have to think about a situation and draw the conclusion that we could get hurt in some way. Once we have thought this once, it can happen a lot more quickly the next time, because of our highly developed capacity for learning. So, the first time you underestimate how hot that dish really is and try to take it out of the oven without oven gloves on will usually also be the last time! This illustrates another principle: when an experience is highly aversive (painful or upsetting), we learn extremely rapidly to avoid a repeat experience.

This explains why we have to watch our children so carefully and teach them about danger. They aren't born knowing that the road is dangerous or the iron is hot. They *learn* to associate danger with certain situations. Depending on how acute the danger or how unpleasant the experience, they may learn quickly or slowly. But, once they have learned that a situation is dangerous, they will react automatically to that situation with fear and the flight or fight response. In the same way, having once learned that a red traffic light means 'stop', we respond automatically. We don't have to waste time trying to remember what a red light means each time we encounter one!

Animals, too, can learn to fear certain situations. We see this in cases where animals have been mistreated. They may come to fear humans, or perhaps an object they have been beaten with. Sometimes animals can develop anxiety problems after other types of traumatic experience, too. For example, when I moved my cat to our new home, I kept her indoors for a week. Unfortunately, on her very first foray into her new backyard, the dog next door threw itself against the fence barking loudly at her. She was terrified, probably because there hadn't been any dogs in her old neighbourhood, and she developed agoraphobia—she wouldn't leave the house willingly. I had to desensitise her by taking her outside with me for gradually increased periods of time. The treatment was successful and eventually she roamed quite freely and didn't seem to be worried at all by the neighbour's dog.

Although animals can learn to fear some situations, this reaction is always linked to physical threat. Humans can perceive different types of threat in their environment—that is, not just physical threats like fire or accidents or being attacked. Humans can also feel threatened by what they can imagine happening, and by non-physical types of threats.

In particular, humans can become anxious about potential losses. We can worry about losing our jobs, our health, our reputation and our loved ones. We can worry about all sorts of bad things that *could* or *might* happen. Problems arise when we start perceiving threats that don't really exist, or that have a very remote chance of occurring. We can start to experience 'false alarms'.

Anxiety disorders are caused by too many false alarms. I will discuss this in more detail later, because it's the key to understanding your own anxiety.

Does anxiety have survival value?

Many authors have speculated over the years about the role of anxiety, and many people wonder whether anxiety is more common in modern life. The flight or fight response appears to have the preservation of life as its main purpose, conferring the ability to take rapid evasive or repulsive action in the face of physical danger. This has led to the suggestion that 'survival of the fittest' may favour those who can perceive and react to a threat quickly, thereby avoiding death. There could be some advantages to being prone to anxiety!

Other writers have noted that women have higher rates of anxiety than men, and have suggested that this may represent an inherent tendency for women to perceive threat more readily. This could have survival value given that women have historically been most involved in caring for and protecting the young. Being able to appreciate a threat early could increase the chances of escape. On the other hand, given that men have had to do more of the physical fighting, it would be an advantage for them to be less easily frightened.

So is anxiety more common now? We really don't know for sure. It would be hard to argue that life is more threatening or dangerous than in the past, although there may be more of some types of stresses (for example, time pressure and the pressure to process and master large volumes of knowledge). It may also be that there is a greater awareness of anxiety and its treatment, so more people are recognising their anxiety for what it is.

HOW MUCH ANXIETY IS TOO MUCH?

Most people are good judges of whether they suffer too much anxiety. If you realise that you worry about things that most people don't, if you feel anxious much of the time, if you experience panic attacks or spend a lot of time worrying about the possibility of having a panic attack, then you have too much anxiety. Too much anxiety interferes with your ability to enjoy life or lead life the way you'd like to. It can put stress on your relationships, on your ability to look after the family and perform well at work.

You may have what mental health professionals call an *anxiety disorder* if you frequently suffer levels of anxiety that are excessive, out of proportion to the actual threat, and which interfere with your enjoyment of life and your social or occupational functioning. In most cases, for it to be severe enough to be called an anxiety disorder, symptoms will have had to be present for weeks to months. Bear in mind that you can have some of the symptoms of one or several of these anxiety conditions without necessarily having a *disorder*, in the same way that you can have a cough and fever without having pneumonia. Doctors will call the condition a disorder if the symptoms match a recognised list and are severe enough to cause disability or significant distress.

Although there are features that are common to all anxiety disorders—such as excessive and inappropriate triggering of the flight or fight response—a number of distinct patterns of anxiety have been recognised. This has resulted in the identification of seven specific anxiety disorders, characterised by different psychological and behavioural symptom patterns, and with minor differences in physical symptoms. Appropriate treatment strategies have now been developed for each of these symptom patterns, which is why we make some effort to distinguish them. The symptom patterns that define each of the anxiety disorders are described in the next chapter.

Chapter Two

ANXIETY DISORDERS

Psychiatrists and psychologists distinguish a number of patterns that excessive anxiety can take, and hence have described a number of different anxiety disorders. The currently recognised anxiety disorders are:

- generalised anxiety disorder
- obsessive compulsive disorder
- post-traumatic stress disorder
- social anxiety disorder (social phobia)
- panic disorder
- agoraphobia
- specific phobia.

To qualify as a 'disorder', the anxiety will usually have been present for some time. High anxiety can also occur as a reaction to stressful events, in which case it may be called an 'adjustment disorder'. This will usually settle quite quickly once the stress is resolved or the person adapts to the stress.

Defining anxiety disorders

In order to facilitate research into anxiety and other psychological illnesses, it is important that doctors and researchers are sure they are all referring to the same patterns of symptoms. If researchers in the Netherlands defined panic disorder differently to Australian researchers—and their definitions were different again to those of researchers in the United Kingdom and the United States—a lot of time and effort would be wasted. We wouldn't be sure whether their results could be applied to our patients, and vice versa. It's a bit like the need for the whole world to agree on how long a marathon is. In psychiatry we haven't quite managed to get one world standard yet, but we've agreed on two systems and most researchers use both so that any clinician anywhere in the world can interpret the results for their patients. The World Health Organization developed the *International Classification of Diseases*, currently in its tenth revision (ICD-10). This defines criteria for all diseases, including psychological illness. The *Diagnostic and Statistical Manual of Mental Disorders*, currently in its fourth revision (DSM-IV), was developed in the United States specifically for psychological disorders. This is the reference most commonly used in Australia for defining the symptoms that make up any given psychological illness, and has been used as the basis for the descriptions given in this book.

GENERALISED ANXIETY DISORDER

Generalised anxiety disorder (GAD for short) is the worrier's illness. If you have GAD you spend much of your day worrying. Your loved ones may say of you that if you don't have something to worry about, you'll find something!

In most cases this will be a tendency you've had since childhood. It may get better or worse depending on the stresses present in your life, but it rarely goes away for long. The worry leads to insomnia, an inability to relax, feeling tense and edgy, and often irritable and jumpy. If these symptoms have been present for at least six months and are causing significant distress or interference in your life, you probably have GAD. As this book is primarily concerned with this disorder, we will discuss it in more detail in the next chapter.

OBSESSIVE COMPULSIVE DISORDER

This anxiety disorder, often abbreviated to OCD, is characterised by distressing thoughts or images of harmful possibilities that seem beyond the sufferer's ability to control. These are referred to as obsessions. Typical examples include recurrent thoughts that the sufferer has come into contact with germs or contamination of some sort; that they may have failed to lock a door or turn off an appliance, or fears they may somehow lose control of themselves and attack someone. The sufferer may experience images of the house burning down or a loved one physically injured. Obsessions cause the sufferer to fear that something terrible will happen, and are usually accompanied by compulsions.

Compulsions are actions that an individual feels compelled to perform in order to reduce the risk that the harmful possibility of the obsession will actually happen. So, to use a common example, an individual may suffer from an obsession about catching an illness from touching buttons and doorknobs that others have handled. They will naturally try to avoid this, but if unable to do so, they will feel a strong and almost irresistible urge to wash their hands immediately afterwards. They feel as if this will reduce the risk of any possible infection or harm.

The obsession often takes the form of unreasonable but maddening doubt. This is generally the case for individuals with obsessions about doors being locked or appliances turned off. The obsession may take the form of a nagging worry—'Did I lock the door?' or 'Did I turn off the stove?'—often occurring once they are down the road or on the way to the bus stop.

For the person with OCD, it is all too easy to find some room for doubt. It is *possible* that they could have forgotten to lock the door, and therefore *possible* that the house could be robbed, and it would be all their fault ... and hence they experience a strong urge to go back and check that the door is locked. It seems a small price to pay for peace of mind.

The problem is that checking once is rarely enough. In addition, there is a level at which the individual *knows* that they have locked the door—it is just the remote possibility that they may not have done so that compels them to go back and check, even while they realise it is probably unnecessary. Most sufferers know that their concerns are exaggerated and unrealistic, but because they find it almost impossible to resist the compulsions, they find themselves trapped in a vicious circle. As you will see, there can be similarities between the concerns of persons with OCD and GAD.

The good news is that OCD responds very well to treatment. Treatment approaches that have been proven to be effective include certain antidepressant medications that increase the level of the body's own serotonin, an important neurotransmitter (a chemical which facilitates communication from one cell to another in the brain); and cognitive behaviour therapy (CBT for short). In CBT a sufferer is supported and encouraged to resist the compulsions they experience in response to their obsessions. Although this is difficult to do, eventually the obsessions and compulsions are considerably weakened and the patient experiences great relief from the OCD. Medication and CBT may be used together.

Many people experience an occasional doubt about the door being locked or the iron being turned off, and have a corresponding urge to check. This is easily differentiated from OCD, where the doubt and the urge to check—or wash, or whatever the compulsion may be—feels like it is taking over the sufferer's life. 'Normal' doubts are mild, and soon fade. Many people won't even bother to check, but if they do, a quick check suffices. The person with OCD may need to repeat the checking (or other ritual) over and over and over.

The Australian Bureau of Statistics conducted a household survey of more than 10 000 adults in 1997, the Australian

National Survey of Mental Health and Wellbeing. It found that in a 12-month period, 0.4 per cent of Australians reported symptoms consistent with a diagnosis of OCD. Men and women are affected about equally.

POST-TRAUMATIC STRESS DISORDER

Most people have heard of post-traumatic stress disorder, or PTSD, usually in connection with ex-servicemen or survivors of natural disasters, torture or terrorism. PTSD also occurs after traumatic experiences, such as car accidents and physical or sexual assault. Generally, the trauma needs to be of sufficient severity that the individual feels their life is in danger. Naturally, most individuals would experience some element of shock and distress after such an experience, but in a minority of individuals the reaction is very severe and does not gradually settle over the ensuing weeks and months as is normally the case.

PTSD is characterised by persistent sleep disturbance, often with recurring nightmares of the event. The individual tends to be jumpy and irritable. They are extremely sensitive to any experience or situation that reminds them in any way of the traumatic event, and usually try to avoid such reminders. They also experience *flashbacks*—vivid, extremely realistic images of the event that occur with no warning, cannot be controlled or prevented, and result in a surge of anxiety or terror as intense as if the event was occurring again. No matter how long ago the experience actually occurred, it feels like it was just yesterday. The individual usually finds that outside of these flashbacks they feel emotionally numb. There is commonly a withdrawal from social interaction.

Treatments for PTSD may include antidepressant medication and CBT. In the case of PTSD, the CBT involves teaching the patient ways to control the anxiety response and then encouraging them to very gradually begin deliberately confronting triggers and reminders of the event. This is called desensitisation, and it progressively wears down the anxiety and reduces the ability of triggers to cause an anxious reaction.

In the 1997 survey, 4.2 per cent of women and 2.3 per cent of men had experienced post-traumatic stress disorder in the preceding 12 months.

PANIC DISORDER

Panic disorder is characterised by recurrent panic attacks, or a fear of having a panic attack, which has been present for at least the last four weeks. Panic attacks are defined in the fourth edition of the *Diagnostic and Statistical Manual of Mental Disorders* as:

A discrete period of intense fear or discomfort, in which four (or more) of the following symptoms developed abruptly and reached a peak within ten minutes:

- palpitations, pounding heart, or accelerated heart rate
- sweating
- trembling or shaking
- sensations of shortness of breath or smothering
- feeling of choking
- chest pain or discomfort
- nausea or abdominal distress
- feeling dizzy, unsteady, lightheaded, or faint
- derealisation (feelings of unreality) or depersonalisation (being detached from oneself)
- fear of losing control or going crazy
- fear of dying
- paraesthesias (numbness or tingling sensations)
- chills or hot flushes.

Reprinted with permission from the *Diagnostic and Statistical Manual of Mental Disorders*, Text Revision, Copyright 2000, American Psychiatric Association.

A panic attack is very frightening because symptoms can easily be mistaken for serious physical illness. For example, the pounding heart can seem like a heart attack, while dizziness may seem like a sign of impending stroke. Treatment involves assisting the individual to recognise the symptoms as being those of the flight or fight response, rather than a serious physical illness, and then use anxiety management strategies, such as breathing control techniques, to control the panic. In resistant cases or where CBT is not available antidepressants may be prescribed.

In the Australian population survey, panic disorder was reported by 0.6 per cent of males and 2 per cent of females over the preceding 12 months.

AGORAPHOBIA

Many people have grown up thinking agoraphobia is 'a fear of open spaces'. This is not entirely accurate, since many individuals with agoraphobia also fear being alone. The confusion may have arisen as a misinterpretation of the meaning of *agora*. This was the ancient Greek term for 'an assembly', which later came to refer to the place of assembly. Although this could be any open space, it was particularly associated with the marketplace. It is really more about crowded places than open spaces. Agoraphobia, in fact, is the fear of having a panic attack in a situation where escape would be difficult or it might be hard to get help. Hence, a crowded marketplace—or our modern day equivalent, the shopping mall—may indeed be anxiety provoking. The crowds and the confusing maze of shops and halls, combined with the knowledge that the exit may be a long way away or hard to find, can make some people feel acutely anxious or fearful. As a result, sufferers begin avoiding situations that trigger their fear.

Commonly avoided situations include shops, public transport, driving, being alone or being too far from a doctor or hospital. Agoraphobia is most effectively treated with CBT. This will include education about the flight or fight response so that the individual understands the true cause and meaning of their symptoms and can control their fears that something is seriously wrong. It also includes instruction in anxiety-management techniques, and a program of graded exposure that will gradually see them confront feared situations.

In the Australian national survey, approximately 0.7 per cent of Australian men and 1.5 per cent of Australian women reported symptoms of agoraphobia over the preceding 12 months. Agoraphobia thus affects women twice as commonly as men; while women are three times more likely to experience panic disorder.

SOCIAL ANXIETY DISORDER (SOCIAL PHOBIA)

Individuals with social anxiety disorder, also known as social phobia, are fearful of being in social situations. Often they themselves are not sure why, but deep down there is usually a fear of being embarrassed somehow. The individual with social phobia may fear doing or saying something embarrassing, looking foolish or inept, or just looking more anxious than they think is normal. They fear that others may think less of them. Whereas sufferers of panic disorder and agoraphobia are most fearful of symptoms that seem to imply a physical illness, those with social phobia worry most about the symptoms of anxiety that may be visible to others.

Hence, the most upsetting physical symptoms of anxiety in this disorder are blushing, sweating, shaking and trembling. Sufferers may also worry about their voice shaking. Some worry about getting so anxious they might vomit while others worry much more than normal about things like passing wind or having a rumbling stomach. The range of feared social situations is varied. The most commonly feared situation in social phobia is public speaking. Interestingly, many people without social phobia are also very anxious about public speaking. However, those with social phobia will usually have other feared situations, such as parties and social gatherings, public transport, shops, eating in public, writing or signing their name when others may be watching, or using the telephone. In addition, their anxiety will be so severe as to cause distress or interfere with their social or occupational functioning. Some social anxiety is normal. When it seems to take over your life it becomes a disorder.

In contrast to those with agoraphobia, individuals with social phobia are usually most comfortable when on their own. Social phobia responds well to CBT and to antidepressants.

The Australian national survey data indicate that social phobia affects about 2.7 per cent of the population, with women affected only slightly more than men.

SPECIFIC PHOBIAS

Some people have fears of quite specific objects or situations, such as heights (acrophobia), plane travel, spiders (arachnophobia), small spaces (claustrophobia), deep water or storms. Such phobias are thought to be common and are usually not disabling. Most people can live a normal life and either not come into contact with their feared situation or object, or find ways to avoid it. A person is more likely to seek treatment if their phobia suddenly starts to interfere with their life. For example, the person with a phobia of heights whose office relocates from the first floor to the forty-first floor may now have a problem. Specific phobias are effectively treated with CBT.

You may have observed that generalised anxiety disorder can have elements of many of these disorders. In particular, the nature of the sufferer's worries may overlap with many of the above concerns. However, people with GAD generally have fewer panic attacks and less concern about the physical effects of panic. They also don't particularly fear crowds and are not excessively socially anxious. They do not have the single focus seen with obsessions in OCD, even though they may have a tendency to check things. There are also a number of features that make GAD quite distinct from other anxiety disorders. We will explore these in the following chapter.

Chapter Three

GETTING TO GRIPS WITH GAD

GAD, or generalised anxiety disorder, was shown in the recent survey of more than 10 000 Australian adults to be the most common anxiety disorder in the Australian community, with 3.6 per cent of adults affected in any 12-month period. Overseas studies have also shown that GAD is very common. So if you have excessive worry and chronic anxiety you are not alone. Men and women are affected almost equally. This is in contrast to panic disorder, agoraphobia and depression, which tend to affect about twice as many women as men. It seems that men are just as good at worrying as women!

THE CAUSES OF GAD

We still don't know for sure what causes GAD, but we have put together some pieces of the puzzle. In psychiatry we have made progress in studying what we call the 'heritability' of disorders, or how they run in families. We have not yet managed to identify any specific genes that cause anxiety, but we do have some understanding of the temperamental factors that predispose to anxiety. It also seems that people can inherit a general tendency to anxiety and depression, though perhaps not specifically to GAD. Temperamental traits are felt to be 'hardwired'. That is, they are present at birth—a result of genetic factors—rather than being something learned. Hence, we refer to them as 'biological' factors. When there is a family history of anxiety, or there is evidence of the temperamental traits that have been associated with anxiety (such as heightened reactivity, discussed below), we say there is an underlying 'biological vulnerability' to anxiety.

The nature of this vulnerability is still being explored. However, it is thought that one significant aspect may be a heightened reactivity to environmental events, especially those of a potentially threatening nature. Such individuals show a tendency to experience a greater than average level of arousal in response to a perceived threat. (Arousal may be thought of as our level of alertness and awareness of our environment. Individuals with a high level of arousal may be jumpy, irritable and find it hard to relax or get to sleep.)

To illustrate this, imagine two people sitting in their respective homes reading the weekend newspaper. One of these individuals is reading the paper when there is an explosion next door. The reader looks up vaguely and says, 'Oh … Was there a noise?' Now imagine our other reader. A car backfires several blocks away and the second reader jumps up in panic, yelling, 'Call the police! There's a bomb!'

In other words, some people perceive a threat more readily and react more quickly and strongly to this threat. Research has also shown that there may be a greater tendency to perceive relatively minor stressful events and situations as more threatening than they actually are. In everyday terms, such people might be described as 'highly strung', and may also display a heightened emotional responsiveness. This seems to be part of their temperament, that is, something they're born with.

Individuals with these characteristics are at higher risk of anxiety disorders. The form that the anxiety takes may be determined mostly by the nature of the stresses or perhaps personality style.

We have also been able to look for 'risk factors' for GAD, things within the individual or the environment that seem to be associated with a higher risk of having GAD. If a first degree relative—a parent, brother or sister—has an anxiety disorder, there is a higher risk of having an anxiety disorder yourself. This appears to be the case whatever type of anxiety problem your relative may have. It is also common that people with GAD may suffer from other types of anxiety at times.

The higher risk that runs in some families seems to have more to do with passing on the biological vulnerability than to any modelling of anxious behaviour. In other words, it's not so much that children learn to be anxious from their parents, but probably rather that they inherit the biological tendency to heightened reactivity, which in turn predisposes to anxiety.

Some research into social phobia, including that by Professor Kenneth Kendler and colleagues in the United States using data obtained from twins, has shown that about 40 to 60 per cent of the cause of social phobia was due to genetic factors. About 30 per cent was due to environmental factors and experiences outside the family, and only a very small contribution came from family environmental factors.

GAD may also be more likely to develop after stressful life events. There is some evidence that sufferers of GAD are somewhat more likely than average to have experienced the loss of or separation from a parent in childhood. There has not yet been much research in this area and we still don't know what role other types of traumas and stresses, such as physical or sexual abuse, may have. It is known that survivors of child physical or sexual abuse commonly experience high levels of anxiety and depression in adulthood, but as yet we do not know of any specific link to GAD.

So to summarise, current thinking is that GAD may develop in response to life stresses in individuals who are already predisposed to anxiety through a highly reactive threat–response system. This is probably genetically determined. At this stage we don't really know enough about the causes of GAD to be able to give advice about avoiding it. However, we do know quite a lot about controlling it, and this is where you can most usefully direct your energy.

GAD: the facts

- It is estimated that somewhere between 3 and 10 per cent of people will suffer from GAD at some time in their life. The National Survey of Mental Health and Wellbeing referred to in the previous chapter showed that in the 12 months prior to being interviewed, approximately 2.4 per cent of men and 3 per cent of women suffered from GAD.
- It seems likely that GAD has a gradual onset in the late teens to late twenties. It may be that initial episodes are more short-lived, lasting for less than the six months required by the DSM-IV (see page 14). People seem more likely to seek help for their GAD in their twenties and beyond, perhaps once they realise it isn't going to go away by itself.
- Some people will have continuous symptoms, while in others severe anxiety and excessive worry will come and go. GAD tends to fluctuate in severity, often in relation to life stresses. Most people will remain prone to excessive worry throughout their lives, and continue to have episodes of worry that interfere with normal life—unless they learn to control it.

SYMPTOMS OF GAD

The defining feature of GAD is worry—constant, intrusive worry that may make it hard to concentrate on other things. Alternatively, having something else to focus on may sometimes help a sufferer distract themself from their worry. Most people who worry too much will say that it's been a part of their personality for as long as they can remember. While the worry can seem completely justified at the time, once the stress is past most sufferers readily acknowledge that their worry was out of proportion to the real chance of something going wrong. This exaggerated fear of a bad or even devastating outcome is what lies behind the worry for most sufferers.

Some people get appendicitis, and some get tonsillitis, but what worriers have in common is what I call 'what-if-itis'. 'What if my husband has had an accident?' 'What if I make the wrong choice and everyone has a terrible time?' 'What if this headache is really a brain tumour?' 'What if I can't cope?' Your thoughts may not always occur exactly as 'what ifs', but if you think about it, this is what many of them are actually saying.

For most people, it turns out that the worry is really about the fear that something bad may happen—someone getting sick, loss of money or job security, damage to their reputation in others' eyes, loss of a relationship. But more than this, it is about not knowing for sure what will happen. Many people are more bothered by the possibility of something bad happening, and by not knowing for sure that things will be okay, than they would be if something actually did go wrong. In fact, many of the worriers I have known have told me that in reality they do cope when things go wrong, but they find it hard to cope with that period of uncertainty before it is clear how things will turn out.

CONSEQUENCES OF GAD

In GAD the sufferer's anxiety is chronic, and results in a range of physical consequences including constant fatigue, poor sleep, muscle tension and headaches. It also leads to irritability, difficulty concentrating, and often a sense of being out of control.

People with GAD are at risk of becoming depressed. This may reflect an increased risk for depression that goes hand in hand with an increased risk for anxiety, or it may occur as a result of the ongoing distress caused by the symptoms of GAD. Many people who suffer from GAD will also suffer from one or more other anxiety disorders through their life, probably as a result of the biological vulnerability that is common to all the anxiety disorders.

Because of the highly unpleasant nature of the anxiety and inability to relax, there can be a risk of turning to alcohol or tranquillisers to relieve the problem. Tranquillisers of the benzodiazepine type—such as Valium, Xanax, Ativan and Serepax—are not the best long-term treatment for anxiety because they can produce sedation, impair reaction times, interfere with memory and interact in potentially harmful ways with alcohol. They also result in physiological and psychological dependency or addiction. This results in an increase in anxiety when there is an attempt to discontinue the medication.

It must be stressed that *benzodiazepine medications should never be abruptly stopped.* There is a risk that this will result in seizures (convulsions or fits). When I see people who are currently taking benzodiazepines, but who want to find a better solution, I first give that person some strategies to help reduce the anxiety so that they have something to take the place of the tranquilliser. When the sufferer is starting to feel some confidence in their psychological strategies, we begin a slow, structured, gradual reduction plan for the tranquilliser.

If the anxiety is too severe to respond to the psychological strategies alone, then I might suggest an antidepressant, and we would wait for this to start to have some effect before beginning the gradual reduction in the benzodiazepine. Your family doctor can give advice and guidance on this issue.

Similarly, the difficulty many people have sleeping may lead to being dependent on sleeping tablets, even though for most people their effectiveness wears off quite quickly. The good news is that there are effective non-drug strategies for improving the quality of sleep. These are described in detail in chapter sixteen.

THE MANY FACES OF GAD

Even though we've looked at the symptoms and some of the consequences, you may still be wondering whether GAD is the correct diagnosis for your pattern of worry. Every person will have slightly different triggers and responses, so let's look at some of the ways GAD can manifest itself, using case studies for illustration. All these cases are based on real-life problems and worries that my patients have described to me over the years, but I have changed names and personal details to protect their identity. Later on in the book we will examine each case and the person's treatment in more detail, but for now, just see whether you can recognise yourself in any of these stories.

Matt's story

Matt is a 28-year-old junior executive in a large, global company. To improve his chances of advancement he studied for an MBA. Before joining the firm Matt had graduated near the top of his class at university, and he knows that some of his drive and his success comes from his tendency to worry—about doing well, about details, about possible problems. While Matt was waiting for the results of his MBA final exams, he became extremely worried that he might have failed. The MBA had been very demanding for Matt, who was also trying to balance work commitments and his relationship with his partner Debbie, and Toby, their 12-month-old son. He wasn't able to study for his final exams as much as he would have liked, and this left him feeling nervous about his level of knowledge. The more he thought about the questions the more he became convinced that he had completely omitted important pieces of information in his answers and was going to fail. He couldn't stop thinking about what this would mean for him. Matt is acutely aware of the competition for his current position, let alone for advancement. His employer had supported his study and he felt it would be humiliating to fail, and his employer would be so annoyed he would terminate Matt's employment. He would never get another job as good as this one and would find himself washed up at the age of 28. Matt couldn't sleep for worry, couldn't eat, couldn't relax, was irritable with Debbie and quite intolerant of Toby's crying. He believed his job performance was suffering, which only exacerbated his fear of losing his job.

When Matt got his final results he found that he was in the top 15 per cent of his class. He thought back and realised that as far back as high school, and throughout university, he had panicked about his exam results, always managing to convince himself he'd failed only to find that he had scored highly. Somehow he's never learned how to give himself the benefit of the doubt, or to wait and see before assuming the worst. He also realises that this is part of a more generalised tendency to worry unreasonably about unrealistic outcomes.

Matt's story illustrates how easy it can be for some worriers to imagine the worst possible outcome, even when all the facts point to a much more positive result. It also shows how hard it can be for sufferers to tolerate uncertainty.

Another problem that occurs when people worry too much is a tendency to jump to conclusions. Catastrophic assumptions are made, often based on limited information, while completely ignoring any more likely explanations. This was the case with Jenny.

Jenny's story

Jenny is a 37-year-old nurse with two young children, Ben (three) and Lily (five). For many years Jenny has suffered from cluster headaches—painful, migraine-like headaches which tend to occur in 'clusters' over several days to weeks at a time. Jenny saw a neurologist about these headaches when she first started getting them in her early twenties. Initially, she was very worried and thought she might have a brain tumour. The neurologist examined her and also ordered some tests, just to be sure. He concluded that she was suffering from cluster headaches and explained to Jenny that these were a type of migraine. He also prescribed some medication for her to try, but Jenny was too anxious to take it. She worried it might have bad side effects or make her feel even worse.

During her nursing training Jenny learned more about cluster headaches and realised that her symptoms did fit the pattern. But she still couldn't help worrying when they came back that maybe this time it really was a tumour. She would carefully monitor her symptoms and try to compare them with the last episode. Were they worse this time? Were they perhaps a bit different than last time? What if the doctors were wrong? Jenny returned to see her neurologist on several occasions for reassurance and, although he was satisfied with the diagnosis, he sent her for a CT scan of her brain. When this was clear it relieved her anxiety ... for a while.

After Jenny had her children, her anxiety about her headaches became much worse. Now she worried that if it *was* cancer and she died, her children would be left motherless. This made her feel both intensely sad and highly anxious. She couldn't stop worrying that maybe her headaches really were because of a brain tumour. She saw another neurologist (who agreed with the first) and had an MRI scan, the best test doctors have for brain tumours. This was normal, which created great relief ... for a while. But then Jenny worried that maybe even the MRI might have missed something, or been mixed up with someone else's somehow ... that it still wasn't the answer.

Jenny became constantly anxious and distressed. Her family doctor, whom she trusted, suggested that the real problem was not a brain tumour, but being unable to control her worry about the headaches. As a nurse Jenny also realised that her doubts about her test results were unreasonable, and she agreed to see whether something could be done about her anxiety.

By far the most likely explanation for Jenny's symptoms is that they represent cluster headaches—as two neurologists, her family doctor and the results of sophisticated medical tests have suggested—and not a brain tumour. But some readers may be thinking that it *could* still be a brain tumour, and, yes, that is possible—extremely unlikely but possible. However, you know that most people would be totally reassured by the expert opinions and test results, and would no longer suffer distressing worry. In chapter five we will discuss the nature of worry in more detail, and in chapters six to ten we will talk about how to begin controlling this worry.

Jenny's worry also fits a common pattern of excessive health anxiety. Many people become unreasonably worried about having an illness or getting sick. Some people, like

Tom (below), have had a serious illness in the past and worry about a recurrence. Others, like Jenny, worry about something they have heard about and fear. Excessive health anxiety is distressing and leads many people to frequent visits to the doctor and avoidance of many everyday activities.

Tom's story

Tom is a 54-year-old teacher, married with four adult children. He prided himself on his level of fitness. He had maintained a trim physique his whole life. He and his wife, a physiotherapist, had always been very health conscious. They had never smoked and emphasised a healthy diet to the whole family. Tom coached soccer for his school, and was himself a keen amateur sportsman, playing football, tennis and golf. Tom also ran four times a week, and had done so for years. He did this to promote his health and cardiovascular fitness. One day Tom noticed that he seemed to have much more trouble covering one of his usual running routes; he seemed tired and lacking in energy. He put it down to a stressful week at work. However, over the next few weeks, Tom had other similar experiences. Sometimes he felt so unwell—dizzy and breathless, with his heart beating very fast—that he had to stop and sit down, and could only walk back home. Tom mentioned it to his wife who urged him to see the doctor. He kept thinking it was just a virus or stress, and would get better. But eventually even Tom had to admit there was something wrong. He went to see his general practitioner, who was instantly alarmed and strictly forbade him to do any physical exercise until the problem was sorted out. He arranged an appointment with a cardiologist for the very next day. The cardiologist was also concerned by Tom's symptoms, and arranged for investigations. Tom's problem was diagnosed as a serious arrhythmia, an irregularity of his heartbeat. He was admitted to hospital for treatment. The laboratory technician arranging further investigations on the cardiologist's orders told Tom he was lucky to be alive, because 'you could have dropped dead at any time with this type of arrhythmia'.

Tom's condition was successfully treated with surgery. The cardiologist was confident the problem had been fixed, although he could not say why it had happened in the first place. It was 'just one of those things'. He said he would review Tom in a week to be sure. At the review the cardiologist was beaming. 'All fixed', he said. He told Tom he could go back to all his usual activities. But Tom found himself worrying about the problem coming back. How could the cardiologist be so sure it was fixed? He could have died! He shouldn't have ignored his symptoms; in future, he would be very, very careful. Tom stopped exercising completely. He checked his pulse several times a day, and avoided the least exertion. He felt anxious and miserable and lost much of his enjoyment of life.

Tom was referred to me by his general practitioner, who wrote in his referral letter: 'Unfortunately, his heart has taken over his life.'

Even though Tom had been assured his problem was fixed, he had been so frightened by what *could have* happened that he could not easily forget it. His fright was more intense because he had believed that his totally healthy lifestyle would protect him from harm. But he was not in control, as he had thought. The unexpected could happen. As a result, he greatly modified his behaviour in ways that only reinforced his anxiety.

Some people have particular areas of worry, like Jenny and Tom, but others worry about everything.

Rosita's story

Rosita, 72, describes herself quite cheerfully as 'a born worrier'. However, her cheerfulness disguises a lifelong problem with anxiety that has made it difficult for her to enjoy her life. 'I've had a good life, doctor,' she said, 'which is why I feel so bad about this worry—there's no *reason* for it. My daughter said there are treatments now and I should come along and get something done about it.'

Rosita's pattern of worry began in childhood. Despite being a much-loved child in a stable, caring family, she was always a nervous child. She was anxious about going to school and frequently complained of headaches and stomach aches, so her mother often kept her home. Rosita was cautious about trying new things and fearful of getting hurt. She would become very upset and anxious before anything out of the usual routine, either at home or at school. She missed so much school she found it hard to keep up, and left at the age of 14. She was too anxious to get a job and so helped her older sister with babysitting so her sister could work in the small mixed business store she ran with her husband. She met her own husband at the church she attended each week and married at the age of 18, beginning her family soon after. Her husband was a bookkeeper who later studied accounting and eventually worked for a small but stable company. His income allowed them to buy a house and educate the children as they wished, without Rosita having to work. He always managed the money to save her the worry.

Rosita was anxious about her children, but had great support from her mother and several older sisters. Nevertheless, she worried enormously whenever they were ill, easily convincing herself that they were going to die. She would have visited her doctor frequently, if her mother and sisters hadn't been able to reassure her and convince her to give an illness time to improve. Her first tendency was to overprotect her children, and only with her husband's firm encouragement was she able to let them do things she'd never have dreamed of doing as a child: school camps, sleepovers at friends, trips away with relatives. Rosita always worried a lot about the future. Would the children be happy? Would they find a partner as loving as her own husband? What if they moved away from her as all the young people were doing now?

Whenever Rosita had some type of event on the calendar, she worried about the things that could go wrong. She would spend much of her day anticipating problems and how she would respond if they happened. She would ask her family for their advice and opinion, but wasn't really reassured because they didn't seem to worry enough. Holidays away were a nightmare for Rosita because of all the planning she felt she had to do and her worry about things going wrong. She also felt the need to check things over and over to be sure that everything was under control. She felt constantly tired, and slept poorly much of her life, taking hours to get to sleep because of all the worries running around her mind. Rosita passed up many opportunities to get involved in activities outside of the home because of her fears that they would be too stressful. She would say, instead, that it was because she needed the time for the children and later the grandchildren. Despite her anxieties Rosita was always cheerful and sensitive to others' needs, and was always well liked.

When Rosita's husband died three years ago, her anxiety became much worse. Suddenly she had to deal with so many things that Frank just used to take care of. She worried about making mistakes—with the tax, with all the complex forms and bills that always seemed to come in. She worried much more about her health—what if she had a fall, or if something happened to her at home alone and she couldn't get help? She just couldn't stop worrying about things. When Rosita saw her doctor, she considered the possibility that Rosita might be depressed; however, Rosita felt that if she could only worry less she would feel better. So Rosita went to see a therapist who specialised in cognitive behaviour therapy and learned some strategies to calm her worry. And she did feel much better! 'I wished I'd learned this a long time ago,' she said.

As Rosita's case shows, anxiety often gets much worse at times of change or stress. It can be anxiety provoking to try something new. In general, individuals with GAD find it a bit harder to cope with change than most people do. When things are in a state of change, it is much harder to feel in control and to predict what will happen. This dislike of uncertainty—together with the discomfort it causes—is one of the core features of GAD and will be discussed in more detail in later chapters.

Rosita's story also illustrates the way in which people who worry too much often become so focused on anticipating problems in the future that they can't enjoy the present. In fact, over the years many sufferers have told me, 'I can't relax when things seem to be going well ... it seems too good to be true and I worry that maybe I'm missing something.' This focus on the future and inability to appreciate good things in the present is typical of GAD.

GAD is also concerned with issues of control. All of us are much more comfortable when we feel that our life is reasonably under control and running in a fairly predictable pattern. However, most people also enjoy some change and novelty, and even some unpredictability in their life. This is not the case with GAD. Most sufferers are extremely uncomfortable with change, uncertainty and unpredictability. It is currently felt that many of the symptoms of GAD represent attempts to feel in more control. Hence reassurance-seeking, checking, avoidance of stressful situations, and probably even worrying may be seen as attempts to get in control—by getting an 'expert' opinion, by making sure of things, by attempting to control the level of stress.

All this worry tends to have another effect: hypervigilance. 'Hyper' means too much, and 'vigilance', of course, is about being alert, keeping an eye out for trouble, having our wits about us. Normally, we automatically monitor our environment—or maintain vigilance—at a fairly relaxed level. But in the face of a real or imagined threat we may greatly increase the amount of time and energy we devote to monitoring for danger. In the case of a realistic threat, this is sensible. For example, imagine you are out bushwalking with friends. When you are some distance away from the safety of your car, you notice some smoke on the horizon. Conscious of the dangers of bushfire, you and your friends discuss the situation. You decide that the smoke is not very plentiful and seems to be a long away off. It's probably just burning off, you decide, so you all agree to keep walking but to monitor the situation. You would naturally find yourself feeling perhaps a little anxious, and would check the smoke frequently in order to be alert to any change that might indicate increased danger. This is adaptive and helpful behaviour when there is a realistic threat.

However, excessive monitoring of the environment for potential threats can become counterproductive if you tend to see potential threat in everything, or if you have catastrophised the real degree of threat (as in Matt's case), or if you have jumped to unfounded conclusions (as in Jenny's case). In this case constant monitoring is only going to exacerbate the problem of seeing a threat that isn't really there, and consequently feeling constantly worried and anxious.

Interestingly, people with too much worry and anxiety can also monitor their *internal* environment excessively. In other words, they can become too focused on what is going on inside their body, and become over sensitive to physical symptoms. This almost certainly contributed to Jenny's problems. It is an important aspect of GAD to understand and overcome and will be considered in more detail in chapters fourteen and fifteen.

Too much worry can also lead to problems with procrastination and indecision. Fear of being responsible for making a bad decision is often part of the worry. Stan's case is an example of this.

Stan's story

Stan is 55. He's in a job he doesn't much like, making soft drink deliveries to small supermarkets and corner stores. The company is restructuring and has offered redundancy packages to employees. Stan always said he would take any opportunity to get out, but now he's faced with the opportunity he's not so sure. In fact, he's paralysed with indecision.

When the offer was made, Stan received details of the package and went home to think about it. He talked about it with his wife. She said, 'Whatever you think, Stan.' He talked it over with his accountant. The accountant said that in his opinion everyone was better off working for as long as possible, but that the package was quite generous. As Stan's wife still enjoyed her job as a teacher and intended to work for a few more years, and given that they owned their own home, the accountant felt they would be able to manage even if Stan didn't get another job. He advised Stan to take the package if he wanted to.

The more Stan thought about it, the more confused he felt. He could see pros and cons. The accountant said they'd be okay, but what if they suddenly needed a lot of money for something? What if he couldn't get another job? What if his wife got sick and couldn't work? What if they got into financial difficulties as a result of him leaving work? It would all be his fault. But he hated the job ...

Stan spoke to his family and friends. His adult children said to do what would make him happy, and not to worry about the money. One person pointed out that Stan had been actively looking for another job. Another reminded him that he'd said he thought he could only stick to it for another year or so anyway. Someone else told a cautionary tale about finding it tough living on superannuation benefits. Stan spoke to a friend who had taken a redundancy package and 'never looked back'. He spoke to another who missed his job and felt quite lonely, but his sister pointed out that this friend was divorced and that was why he was lonely.

None of these other opinions seemed to make it any easier for Stan to make a decision. He worried about it constantly. The pros and cons went round and round in his head, but there was no resolution. He lost his appetite and began to sleep poorly. He could talk of nothing else and seemed to be constantly distracted. As the deadline approached he became increasingly distressed. He simply could not make a decision.

Stan worries about all sorts of possible problems and outcomes. His story illustrates how excessive worry about possibilities can make it difficult to make decisions and lead to procrastination.

ARE YOU SUFFERING FROM GAD?

Some of these case studies may seem a little extreme to you, or perhaps you identify with them more than you would like to admit. If you're reading this book you probably suspect that you worry more than most people. We get an idea of how we compare to others just by talking about everyday life experiences, and listening to others. It becomes pretty clear how much most people worry about their health or finances, their job and relationships. We find out how others respond to stress and challenges—whether they tend to expect the worst or not; whether they tend to take unexpected problems in their stride better than we do. So you may already be fairly clear about where you are on the spectrum of worry. For those who would like a more objective measure there is a questionnaire that I often use with my patients. This is the Penn State Worry Questionnaire, which was developed by Professor Thomas Borkovec and colleagues at the Pennsylvania State University (hence 'Penn State'). This questionnaire can also be used to monitor your progress during treatment.

Penn State Worry Questionnaire

Answer all the questions by writing down the number that best corresponds to how you relate to each statement. Then score yourself according to the instructions below.

Decide on the number that best describes how typical or characteristic each item is of you. Record the number next to the item.

1	2	3	4	5
Not at all typical		Somewhat typical		Very typical

___ 1. If I don't have enough time to do everything, I don't worry about it.

___ 2. My worries overwhelm me.

___ 3. I don't tend to worry about things.

___ 4. Many situations make me worry.

___ 5. I know I shouldn't worry about things, but I just can't help it.

___ 6. When I am under pressure, I worry a lot.

___ 7. I am always worrying about something.

___ 8. I find it easy to dismiss worrisome thoughts.

___ 9. As soon as I finish one task, I start to worry about everything else I
have to do.

___ 10. I never worry about anything.

___ 11. When there is nothing more I can do about a concern, I don't worry
about it any more.

___ 12. I've been a worrier all my life.

___ 13. I notice that I have been worrying about things.

___ 14. Once I start worrying, I can't stop.

___ 15. I worry all the time.

___ 16. I worry about projects until they are all done.

- For items 2, 4, 5, 6, 7, 9, 12, 13, 14, 15 and 16 add up the scores next to
the items.
- For items 1, 3, 8, 10 and 11, reverse your score, then add it to the total.
So, if you wrote down:

  1, add 5 to your score.

  2, add 4 to your score

  3, add 3 to your score, etc.

Reprinted from *Behaviour Research and Therapy*, Vol. 28, Borkorec,
'Development and validation of the Penn State worry questionnaire,'
pp. 487–95, Copyright 1990, with permission from Elsevier.

Interpreting your score

You may be relieved to know that it is impossible to score
zero on this questionnaire! The minimum score is 16 and
the maximum score is 80. In general, the higher your score
the more of a worrier you are. In my practice I commonly
see people who score in the seventies. It is considered that if
your score is below 58, your symptoms of worry are
unlikely to be severe; hence, this could be your goal.

Chapter Four

TREATMENT OF GAD

It seems that many people do not seek help for their problems with excessive worry and anxiety. When people do try to get help, most see their family doctor as the first port of call. Unfortunately, the report card for doctors in recognising this condition is not good—not even a pass rate in one study, where only 46 per cent of GAD sufferers were recognised as suffering from the disorder.

Information collected in the Australian National Survey of Mental Health and Wellbeing in 1997 identified a group of people who had experienced worry symptoms severe enough to be diagnosed as generalised anxiety disorder according to DSM-IV criteria at some time in the last 12 months. Colleagues of mine at the University of New South Wales and the World Health Organization Collaborating Centre for Evidence and Health Policy in Mental Health at St Vincent's Hospital in Sydney examined the information survey participants gave the interviewers about their illness and its treatment. Of these individuals with GAD, only 37.6 per cent were receiving treatment, and it was estimated that about half of those people (45.5 per cent) were receiving treatment for which there was no evidence of effectiveness, possibly wasting their time, money and energy. People not receiving treatment were asked the reasons for this. Sixteen per cent wanted the sort of treatment that would have helped them, but said they couldn't get it; and 31 per cent wanted treatment of a sort that probably wouldn't have helped. Fifty-three per cent said they did not think they needed treatment. Bear in mind that this survey only diagnosed GAD when individuals met DSM-

IV criteria requiring that symptoms caused significant distress or interfered with the ability to work and/or function normally in social and domestic roles.

Why would people say they didn't need treatment? One thing that I have observed over the years is how much people change their lifestyle to accommodate their anxiety. They stop taking on big challenges, and try to avoid change or pressure in their life. They might avoid things like travelling too far away on holiday, changing jobs, getting involved in challenging work projects or taking on extra responsibilities at home, school or work. Eventually, this degree of restriction just becomes a way of life, and the person may forget that it isn't what they'd planned. They may just get used to the poor quality sleep, constant tiredness, headaches and other physical symptoms that result from so much worry and forget that these aren't normal! Many people in the survey indicated that they preferred to manage things themselves. It is also quite likely that many people are pessimistic about whether anything could change the way they are.

Hopefully the information in this book will prevent you from being one of the 62 per cent not receiving treatment that could alleviate your worry and anxiety! There *are* effective treatments for excessive worry and anxiety. These have been proven to be effective through well-conducted research and include both medication and psychological strategies.

ANTIDEPRESSANT TREATMENT FOR GAD

Have you ever wondered why antidepressants would be recommended for anxiety? If a person isn't depressed, would they still work? The answer is an unequivocal 'yes'.

Antidepressants, as the name implies, were first developed for use in the treatment of depression, but they were actually an accidental discovery. The first antidepressant was meant to have been a new drug for treating tuberculosis, still a great scourge at the time of research in the 1950s. The drug was not very effective against tuberculosis, but an observant researcher noticed that it seemed to improve the patients' mood. Thus, the first antidepressant was born, and others soon followed.

In the 1970s, researchers began to experiment with using antidepressants to treat panic disorder. When they were found to be effective in reducing panic attacks, they were tried in other anxiety disorders, with equally good results. A further benefit was that their effectiveness didn't rely on producing a sedative effect; in other words, an antidepressant doesn't have to make you sleepy to work on your anxiety.

A number of antidepressants are currently recommended as being the safest, most effective and most practical pharmacological treatments for GAD. The list of anti-depressants that have been shown to work for GAD is frequently updated in the light of new research findings, so ask your doctor or check a reputable website for the latest information. Your doctor will help you to choose the medication that best suits you, if you both decide that this is a treatment option appropriate for you.

Benzodiazepines (see also page 28) are not recommended except for very short periods of time (days to a couple of weeks at the most) to treat overwhelming levels of anxiety that may have developed acutely in response to a particular stress, and that are not settling with psychological strategies and relaxation techniques. This is more likely to be the case for an individual who has not yet sought treatment for their anxiety, as other sufferers will already be taking an effective medication or learning effective psychological strategies and are therefore much less likely to get debilitating levels of anxiety.

If you do start antidepressant medication, it is important to be aware that your doctor will recommend that you take it *for at least six months*. It does not work instantly, but will take two to four weeks to begin to have a noticeable effect. All medications have side effects, but with modern antidepressants these are usually not severe, and many (but not all) of the side effects get better over time. Common side effects include nausea, headache and dizziness (all of which usually go away after a few days); vivid dreams, reduced libido, delayed ejaculation or difficulty achieving orgasm (which don't tend to get better). Most of the newer antidepressants do not cause weight gain. Sometimes the antidepressants seem to make you feel more anxious for the first few days, although this can usually be avoided by starting with only half a tablet for the first few days, or until you feel your body has adjusted to the medication. Some people will feel more alert and may suffer insomnia, others may feel a little sedated; some individuals may experience a dry mouth, increased sweating or tremor. The exact pattern of side effects that will be experienced is quite individual and difficult to predict. Some side effects may occur with one antidepressant but not so much with another.

Serious adverse reactions and side effects are uncommon, but can occur. In most cases detailed information specific to each antidepressant about the risk of serious adverse reactions is available to your doctor. However, some reactions are 'idiosyncratic' and can't be predicted. If you have any concerns, contact your doctor or local health service immediately.

You do need to remember that if you have become hypervigilant not only to your external environment but also to your internal environment (that is, bodily symptoms and sensations), you will be more prone than the average person to notice side effects. In fact, we know that many people experience side effects from taking a sugar pill (see box).

The placebo effect

Good-quality research into the effectiveness of medication requires investigators to compare the response to the medication being studied with the response to a placebo (or 'sugar pill'). The placebo is designed to look exactly like the medication but usually has no active ingredients—indeed, it is often mostly some type of sugar. Neither the investigators nor the patients in the research study know which is the active drug and which is the placebo. It is all done using random computer allocation and codes to disguise who is getting what. Side effects and beneficial effects are measured each week or so as the research trial progresses. At the end of the trial the code is cracked and the effects of the placebo are compared to those of the active tablet. Here is a sample of the findings that were reported for one such medication in the *MIMS Annual* of June 2003. The rate refers to the percentage of people taking that category of pill who experienced the symptom in question.

Side effect	Rate for antidepressant	Rate for placebo
Headache	26.9%	26.7%
Nausea	21.4%	13.2%
Dry mouth	20.0%	12.6%
Insomnia	18.8%	18.9%
Somnolence	17.9%	10.3%
Asthenia	11.5%	11.7%
Sweating increase	11.3%	7.4%
Dizziness	10.3%	10.1%
Palpitations	7.1%	7.4%

Reproduced with permission from MIMS Australia. Copyright MediMedia Australia Pty Limited.

A large number of symptoms were studied—I chose the nine most commonly reported for comparison. What is striking is that many of the most frequently experienced side effects are reported at almost equal rates by both those on sugar pills and those taking the antidepressant. Of this list, only nausea, dry mouth, somnolence and increased sweating were experienced significantly more often by the group taking the antidepressant. This is a real life demonstration of the power of the mind. If we expect to find something, and if we look for it hard enough, we will usually find it. While this can be helpful, it can also cause problems.

The most common side effects of antidepressants are unpleasant but not dangerous. If you experience side effects that don't improve over a week or so, and are too unpleasant to live with, don't just give up. Go back and talk to your doctor and tell him or her about the problems you experienced. There are many other antidepressants to choose from. One word of caution: don't stop your antidepressants suddenly once you become established on them, or you may experience what are called 'discontinuation effects'. Unlike with benzodiazepines, these symptoms are not harmful or dangerous, but they are unpleasant, and can be minimised by stopping your antidepressant gradually. Some antidepressants are more prone to cause these symptoms than others. Typical discontinuation effects include dizziness, nausea and an odd sensation of movement when the head is turned quickly, as if your eyes aren't quite keeping up. Many people also talk of feeling what might best be described as 'seedy', or a bit like having a hangover. Sometimes these symptoms can be experienced even when a daily tablet is forgotten. They go away quite quickly when the missed tablet (or even a reduced dose) is taken.

What should you expect from your antidepressant?

After two to four weeks you should notice that you feel less anxious and worried. You may find yourself able to sleep better. You should find yourself feeling less on edge. You will still find that worries come into your head, but it should be easier to let go of them. These effects will increase in strength over the next few weeks or so, and after eight to 12 weeks as you continue to take the tablet you might feel like you have only normal levels of anxiety—just like anyone else. This is the ideal outcome. Although as yet there are few studies that have examined the question of remission (complete recovery), the available evidence suggests this may be experienced by approximately 40 per cent of people who choose to take an antidepressant. However, 20 per cent might also be expected to achieve this outcome if they were given a placebo. About 60 to 65 per cent of people who take antidepressants for their anxiety, and 40 per cent who take a placebo, will notice definite improvement while taking the medication in question but not to the point of feeling that their symptoms are no longer a problem.

It is also important to note that antidepressants only work as long as you take them. Most people find that their anxiety comes back once they stop the medication—unless they have learned to control their anxiety. This is why all therapists who specialise in treating anxiety will recommend that sufferers learn strategies to control their anxiety, including stress management, relaxation techniques and cognitive behaviour therapy.

COGNITIVE BEHAVIOUR THERAPY

So far the most effective treatment for anxiety that does not involve medication is cognitive behaviour therapy (CBT). This type of therapy uses both psychological techniques and changes in behaviour. The CBT treatment of GAD has been evolving rapidly over the past few years, and studies on the effectiveness of the newer elements of treatment are in the pipeline. It has been estimated that approximately 50 per cent of people who are treated with CBT will achieve a high level of functioning after treatment. Interestingly, results often improve over time, even after the treatment sessions have ended. CBT may also take a little longer than antidepressant medication to begin to have a noticeable effect.

What is CBT?

CBT is considered a type of psychotherapy, but it differs in several significant ways from the more traditional style of psychotherapy first described by Sigmund Freud. CBT was developed in the 1950s. The two most famous names associated with this style of therapy are Aaron Beck and Albert Ellis (who calls his version rational emotive behaviour therapy, or REBT). CBT is based on the premise that how we feel (our emotional state) has more to do with how we think about ourselves and our world than it has with what actually happens.

To understand this, imagine that three winners are drawn from a travel competition, and each is handed a voucher to fly to Hawaii for a week's holiday for two people. The first person immediately begins to look very worried and a bit shaky; the second person bursts into tears; and the third person smiles very broadly and looks extremely pleased. Now, you might have expected that each person would have reacted like the third person—with evident pleasure. The only way to understand the others' reactions is if you know what they were thinking. It turns out that the first person has a fear of flying, and began to worry about whether they would be able to get on the plane ... and whether it would be safe to travel ... and what if they got sick while they were away ... The second person was left by their partner some time after entering the competition and so burst into tears at the thought of no longer having their partner to share something like this with. The third person is simply thrilled and looks forward to an all-expenses-paid vacation.

CBT aims to help people become more aware of how

their thinking influences their emotional state. They are encouraged to pay particular attention to thoughts that are linked to feeling bad in some way—unreasonably anxious, sad or angry, for example. The next step is to scrutinise the thoughts behind these feelings and decide whether they are realistic and helpful. If not, the individual is encouraged to modify their conclusions so that they better reflect reality. The individual chooses to think about things in a way that is more helpful and supportive to them in coping with stresses and achieving their goals in life.

The therapy incorporates a variety of behavioural strategies, from relaxation and breathing control techniques to a step-by-step confrontation of fear-provoking situations (referred to as 'graded exposure'). It includes pleasant event scheduling (planning to incorporate pleasurable activities into everyday life) exercise and strategies for improving sleep; as well as behavioural exercises developed for specific problems. Behavioural strategies work hand in hand with cognitive strategies. Behaviour can reinforce thinking, and thinking more helpfully can make it easier to do things that are difficult or anxiety provoking.

CBT differs from traditional (psychoanalytic or psycho-dynamic) psychotherapy by focusing on the here-and-now and on making changes for the future. There is relatively little emphasis on understanding the past, so people who have a great need to understand past influences in their lives may be better off trying other forms of therapy. CBT is also a structured therapy, and relies heavily on the work an individual does outside of sessions to put techniques and strategies into practice, rather than on simply talking about problems. It suits people who want to feel more in control and learn strategies to overcome their psychological problems, but it requires a willingness to do 'homework' outside of sessions. This includes writing down thoughts and observations, analysing one's own behaviour and thinking, and making time to practise behavioural and anxiety control exercises.

CBT and GAD

The most established CBT techniques for treating GAD include applied relaxation and structured problem solving. Applied relaxation employs a technique known as progressive muscular relaxation, in which each muscle group in the body in turn is first tensed and then allowed to relax. As simple as it sounds, this technique is effective in reducing arousal and promoting relaxation when practised regularly. It can improve sleep and contribute to a greater sense of feeling relaxed. It will be discussed in detail in chapter five.

Structured problem solving provides a framework for addressing realistic problems and finding potential solutions. When put into practice it can save many hours of unproductive and distressing worry. It will be discussed in more detail in chapter nine.

Cognitive challenging, also referred to as cognitive restructuring or 'straight thinking', is another well-established CBT technique that we will look at in chapter eleven. It can assist worriers to differentiate between realistic and unrealistic worries, and improve their ability to make judgements about the real risks of something going wrong.

I have also included many new cognitive behavioural strategies, which are based on the results of recent research into the nature of GAD. A better understanding of the problem of too much worry is enabling researchers and clinicians to develop promising new treatment techniques. Many of these techniques are so new that there is so far only a small amount of research to support their effectiveness. However, all the strategies included in this book have at least some research evidence showing a positive benefit. Just as importantly, all the strategies in this book have been used successfully by real life worriers who have come to see me in my practice over the years. These individuals have helped me to learn what works best, and to develop and refine these strategies over time. These new cognitive behavioural strategies include techniques for controlling worry and learning to tolerate uncertainty, and will be described in detail in subsequent chapters. Finally, I have also included strategies for improving sleep and making decisions—other difficulties that can be experienced by worriers.

It is important to note that not all readers will find all the techniques helpful. The next few chapters will help you to analyse and better understand your own pattern of worry and anxiety and may help you decide which techniques may be useful to try. It must be stressed that CBT requires consistent practice to be effective. Some of the techniques require you to confront your anxiety and will therefore be quite hard work at times, although you will always be advised to take one manageable step at a time and not to try to master everything at once!

Is it worth all this hard work when you could just take a pill? Yes, for several reasons. The benefits of CBT tend to be longer lasting than the effects of medication. In every anxiety disorder so far studied, patients unfortunately tend to relapse (get their symptoms back) when they stop the medication, unless they have also done some CBT. Additionally, in many cases medication does not completely alleviate symptoms; and it is invariably associated with at least some side effects.

THE BOTTOM LINE: MEDICATION OR CBT?

Without doubt, CBT is a highly effective treatment that will help you to get better and stay better. Whatever other treatments you try, you owe it to yourself to try CBT. Antidepressants can be a helpful adjunctive treatment, and I recommend them in the following circumstances:

- When a person who is very anxious is also significantly depressed: it's just too hard to do CBT when you've got this dual burden.
- When a person is so highly anxious or agitated that they can't really concentrate on anything else, and can't even manage to use the relaxation technique: antidepressants are often very effective at alleviating this highly anxious state. They will take a couple of weeks to start to work and this is one situation where a very brief use of benzodiazepines while a person is waiting for the antidepressants to 'kick in' can be justified.
- When a person is so demoralised by their anxiety that they need something that can be relied upon to work quickly. CBT can be very effective, but you could find it doesn't suit you, and it probably does take a bit longer to start to help than antidepressants, since you first have to learn the techniques, then practise them.

PROFESSIONAL HELP

This book is designed to give you the facts about too much worry, and detailed information on strategies that can help you to control it. However, as with a diet or an exercise program, it can really help to have a personal coach and/or a support network. There are several types of professionals who can offer advice and treatment for anxiety, and advise you on whether your symptoms are consistent with GAD, another anxiety disorder, or some other problem entirely. For example, GAD can easily be confused with obsessive compulsive disorder; it is also common for depression to be associated with high anxiety levels. Your GP, a psychologist or a psychiatrist can make an assessment of your problems and offer advice on treatment.

What's the difference between a psychiatrist and a psychologist?

This is something that confuses a lot of people! To summarise:

A *psychologist* has completed a three- or four-year university degree in the field of psychology. Their qualifications may say B. Psychol. or sometimes B.A. or B.Sc. Some have done further years of study in psychology to obtain a Masters level (M. Psychol.) or Doctorate level (Ph.D.) degree.

A *psychiatrist* trains as a doctor and then goes on to specialise in psychiatry. So they have completed a medical degree at university (MB, BS; MB, ChB; or, in the United States, MD) and then completed further training to specialise in psychiatry. In Australia and New Zealand this training takes a further five years, and qualifies the doctor for Fellowship of the Royal Australian and New Zealand College of Psychiatrists, abbreviated to FRANZCP. A psychiatrist retains the ability to prescribe medication, and is skilled at diagnosing mental problems. In Australia you need a referral from your GP in order to be eligible for Medicare benefits for seeing a psychiatrist.

Your GP is well placed to guide you in what type of treatment may suit you best, whether it is advisable to see a psychiatrist or psychologist, and to recommend someone they think would be helpful to you. You may also get a recommendation from family or friends, or from an anxiety support group regarding an experienced professional in your area. The most important qualification is experience in treating anxiety disorders. If you want to try CBT, look around for someone who has experience in this type of therapy, and preferably specific experience in using CBT to treat anxiety disorders.

This book gives as much practical detail as possible on strategies for mastering your anxiety and worry so that you can get some benefit even if you are working on your own. However, it can be helpful to have the assistance of a professional. They can give advice on tailoring the program to your individual needs, help troubleshoot when strategies don't seem to be working for you, or prescribe medication when this would be helpful. I aim to use this book in therapy with my patients so that they can read more about worry and how to control it, revise what we've discussed in sessions, and have a treatment resource to keep for the future when they are no longer seeing me.

Support groups can be helpful to some people. They can be a source of information and support. If you feel you would like to join such a group, go along for a few meetings and get a feel for the group. Check the following:

- Are the members focused on getting well, or do they just want to talk about how unpleasant their symptoms are?
- Do they have useful advice and accurate information about anxiety?
- Do they get their information from recognised sources such as university clinics or government health departments?

You can find out about support groups in your area by asking your GP, your local community health centre, or by contacting mental health consumer groups such as the Mental Health Association or SANE.

Do you need professional help now?

If you are currently more than mildly depressed, I recommend you see your GP now. This is because moderate to severe levels of depression are likely to prevent you from being able to use the strategies in this book effectively—it's like trying to get fit when you're suffering from severe influenza or recovering from an operation. Depression results in a negative frame of mind that will colour the way you see the world and make it difficult to consider an alternative point of view. This will prevent you from being able to use the cognitive strategies that are described in later chapters of this book, although the de-arousal strategies may still be helpful. Depression can also lead to anxiety, and sometimes this is the real cause of an apparent increase in anxiety symptoms.

The symptoms of depression include the following:

- depressed mood for much of the day on most days over a period of at least two weeks
- disturbed sleep (too little or too much)
- loss of interest or enjoyment of life
- reduced self-esteem and self confidence
- loss of interest in social activities, and social withdrawal
- disturbed appetite
- reduced energy
- reduced concentration
- impairment of memory
- loss of interest in sex
- feeling slowed down in your thinking or movements
- feelings of guilt and worthlessness
- thoughts of suicide.

The last three symptoms are particularly worrisome and are suggestive of a more severe level of depression requiring urgent treatment. In such a case your GP may suggest you take an antidepressant and may also suggest referral to a psychiatrist. If so, follow his or her advice! Psychiatrists are really not so scary, and depression is a treatable illness. In most cases you can be feeling a lot more like your old self within a few weeks. If your old self is too anxious, that can be worked on next!

Chapter Five

TAKING CONTROL OF YOUR ANXIETY AND WORRY

Anxiety causes three main types of symptoms: psychological, physical and behavioural. There is no 'magic bullet' in the treatment of anxiety—no one treatment that can be relied upon to fix the problem. To control your anxiety and worry you will need a range of strategies, all of which can be expected to contribute something to reducing your symptoms. To decide which cognitive behavioural strategies may be effective for you, the first step is to get to know your own pattern of anxiety better.

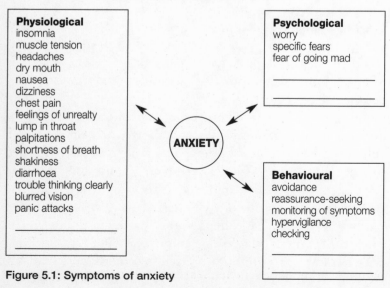

Physiological
insomnia
muscle tension
headaches
dry mouth
nausea
dizziness
chest pain
feelings of unreality
lump in throat
palpitations
shortness of breath
shakiness
diarrhoea
trouble thinking clearly
blurred vision
panic attacks

_____

_____

ANXIETY

Psychological
worry
specific fears
fear of going mad

_____

_____

Behavioural
avoidance
reassurance-seeking
monitoring of symptoms
hypervigilance
checking

_____

_____

Figure 5.1: Symptoms of anxiety

As a first step examine the diagram above and tick the symptoms that affect you. Add any of your own that are not on the list. Subsequent chapters will describe a range of strategies and the sorts of problems each strategy can help. You can then choose the strategies that are appropriate for your own problems with anxiety.

DE-AROUSAL STRATEGIES

Your first step in taking control of your worry is to get started straight away on reducing the severity of any physical symptoms you may have ticked. These physical symptoms occur as a consequence of high levels of arousal associated with hypervigilance and constant anxiety and worry (through the flight or fight response). There are a number of strategies that have been shown to reduce this level of physiological arousal, and we call these de-arousal strategies. They include:

- exercise
- progressive muscular relaxation
- hyperventilation control
- other strategies such as yoga and meditation.

Many people underestimate the value of such strategies— perhaps they seem too simple to be powerful. They also require time, effort and an ongoing commitment, and this is not easy to find when you are leading a busy life and feeling exhausted from your worry.

Exercise

Exercise combats anxiety in a number of ways. Many people have heard of 'endorphins', the body's natural painkiller. These neurochemicals are released in response to exercise and have the additional benefit of relieving stress. More recently, exercise has also been shown to promote the growth of new brain cells, particularly in areas of the brain involved in memory and emotion. Exercise also enhances the quality of sleep. This is, of course, in addition to all the physical benefits of exercise in promoting heart health, controlling weight and keeping bones and muscles strong.

With all these benefits why do so few people exercise regularly? There are probably several reasons. Our lives have become very busy with many people working long hours, often having to spend a considerable time commuting to work. Our kids all do a myriad of extra-curricular activities that require Mum or Dad to be the chauffeur. On top of this many people are trying to study part time. And there's the problem of being unfit. It's much harder to start exercising when you're unfit: there's the tendency to procrastinate ('I'll start tomorrow, one more day won't make any difference.'); and you're more likely to feel a bit stiff and sore at first, which is not much fun. You can't see any immediate benefits, either, which makes it hard to find the motivation to keep at it.

Despite these difficulties, most people want to exercise regularly because of the health benefits. Some of the strategies in the box may help you to get started.

Tips for getting started on an exercise program

- Identify your own personal reasons for wanting to exercise. Identify the goals you would like to achieve. For example, 'lose 5 kilograms' or 'reduce anxiety'. Write these down.
- Remind yourself frequently of your goals and your reasons for wanting to exercise. When you are tempted to start tomorrow or to miss a session, go back and look at your goals.

- Start gradually, and have modest expectations. For example, aim to walk for 15 minutes at a time and to do this three times a week initially. Then gradually increase your goal time, distance or frequency as it gets easier.
- If you can find someone else to exercise with, it increases the chances that both of you will go regularly. It can also be more enjoyable and take your mind off the hard work you're doing.
- When you really don't feel like getting out there, make it easier on yourself, but still go. For example, you might say to yourself, 'Okay, I really don't feel like it today, but I do want to reach my goals and keep up the momentum I've built. So I will go out but I only have to walk for ten minutes today.'
- Keep a record of your exercise sessions. What you did, how far you went, how long you exercised for. Research has shown that record keeping increases the likelihood of sticking to almost any type of program.
- Include a variety of physical activities to reduce your chances of becoming bored.

Any kind of exercise can be beneficial. Walking is probably the easiest and gentlest type of exercise, and can provide all the benefits we're looking for. People who suffer from anxiety would benefit from engaging in some type of de-arousal strategy every day. An example might be to do yoga on Monday and Thursday; walk on Tuesday, Friday and Saturday; and ride the bike with the family on Sunday. Ideally, a person needs three to four aerobic exercise sessions a week to get fit. But don't be daunted by this eventual goal—just get started.

At the end of the day, there is no easy way. You just have to make up your mind to get started and then, like the Nike ad says, 'Just do it!'

Progressive muscular relaxation

There are numerous relaxation tapes available commercially. Most of these involve creative visualisation of some type, and many anxious people find these tapes difficult to use successfully. Fortunately, research has shown that progressive muscular relaxation is an effective technique for reducing anxiety. It has also been shown to result in modest reductions in blood pressure, which is further evidence that it is having a real physiological effect.

Progressive muscular relaxation is an active form of relaxation. That is, it is a skill that requires active practice, and at which you can get better. With regular practice you will become better able to relax and control your level of tension. As your muscles are less tense your blood pressure will lower, your heart won't have to work as hard, and the feedback to your brain of more relaxed muscles will help to reduce the output of stress hormones and your level of arousal.

The technique requires you to alternately tense and relax different groups of muscles around the body. For example, you might begin by curling your toes over, holding this for a couple of breaths, then releasing for a few breaths. Next, move on to the calves and tense these by pointing your toes. Hold for a couple of breaths, then release. Next tense the front of the lower leg by turning your feet up at the ankles. Hold, then release. Importantly, the tension should not be applied too strongly—it's not meant to be painful!

It can be helpful when you first start to practise this technique to have the instructions on a tape or CD to guide you. This has the additional advantage of giving you something to focus on. In fact, your relaxation sessions can give you the opportunity to begin to practise an extremely important skill that will be discussed in more detail in later chapters: attention focusing. The aim is to learn to pay less attention to worries, and to become better at directing your attention to where you choose, rather than finding it hijacked by fears. In order to practise this, as soon as you catch yourself thinking about something other than the relaxation activity aim to gently 'let go' of the thought. Immediately refocus your attention on whatever muscle group you were working on, and back to what is being said on your relaxation tape or CD. The key here is not to become frustrated or upset with yourself about having become distracted, and also to let go of the intruding thought as soon as you become aware your mind has wandered. If you can practise this consistently you will find your ability to ignore unwanted thoughts and worries improves significantly. Some readers will recognise a parallel with meditation techniques in the idea of 'letting go' of thoughts, and indeed this is the same idea. You can see how meditation can be a useful strategy in chronic anxiety and excessive worry.

It takes about two weeks of daily practice before you will see benefits from progressive muscular relaxation. Aim to practise as often as you can, but avoid the 'all or nothing' pitfall of saying, 'Well, I can't practise every day so why bother at all?' Any practice you do is worthwhile, so just do what you can. Each session will take about 25 to 30 minutes of your time: an investment of time in the present for a calmer future.

Note that it is not ideal to try this technique when you are in bed ready to go to sleep, as you will probably fall asleep before completing the practice. Instead, try to find another time of day where you can arrange not to be disturbed for half an hour. This may take some negotiation in a busy household. Some of my patients have arranged to do their practice in work hours, in their office if they have privacy, or sitting in their car somewhere. To reduce the likelihood of falling asleep, do your practice sitting up. It's helpful to be able to rest your head back against something. Don't worry too much about having absolute quiet or a dark room; you can learn to relax under any circumstances. In fact, the better your skill at relaxing the more 'portable' it will become, so that you can achieve a state of relaxation even when you're unable to find a private spot.

Portability of relaxation is achieved through a technique known as applied relaxation, which was first described and studied by Lars-Goran Ost, a Swedish psychologist. In this technique, the time to achieve a state of relaxation is gradually reduced, and the ability to apply the relaxation technique in a variety of settings, even while engaged in other activities, is practised. The first step is to master the basic technique of progressive muscular relaxation, practising initially with a tape or CD, then gradually learn how to achieve the same level of relaxation by giving yourself the prompts without needing the tape or CD. I find most people are happy to get to this level and maintain it, but for those who would like to read more about applied relaxation, the reference for the original research paper by Dr Ost is given in the Bibliography on page 248.

Hyperventilation control

If you frequently feel breathless when you're anxious or worried, or if you experience a lot of dizziness, the chances are you're hyperventilating. Hyperventilation is the technical term for overbreathing—breathing at a rate that is faster or deeper than necessary. Normally the brain controls the level of respiration, automatically matching it to your physiological requirements. It will thus vary automatically depending on whether you are sleeping, reading, doing the housework or exercising. The flight or fight response results in an increase in the rate of respiration, in preparation for an anticipated flight from danger. Hence, many anxious individuals frequently find themselves hyperventilating. Hyperventilation itself can then worsen the symptoms of anxiety as a result of the sufferer feeling breathless. It can also result in dizziness, chest tightness and, in severe cases, muscle spasm.

Are you hyperventilating?

This is easy to measure. Sit quietly for at least ten minutes; then simply count the number of breaths you take in a minute. Breathing in and out counts as one complete breath. You may feel as though your rate has changed because you're focusing on it, but this doesn't actually happen to any great extent.

How many breaths did you take in a minute? A rate of eight to 12 breaths per minute is usually regarded as normal. If your rate was greater than this you are hyperventilating and may benefit from practising a breathing control strategy.

It is also interesting to measure your breathing rate when you are feeling anxious and worried, and then compare it to the rate you measure when you are just sitting and reading.

Hyperventilation tends to be a more prominent problem in panic disorder. However, many people with excessive worry find that they have periods where they become acutely anxious in response to a particular worry, and the breathing control exercise described below can be helpful at these times. It helps by calming the panic so that you can think more clearly and apply the cognitive strategies that you will be introduced to later in the book. The relaxation and breathing control strategies form the foundation of your anxiety management program.

Breathing control technique

The aim is to breathe in a smooth and light way throughout the practice. This is probably in direct contrast to instructions to take deep breaths that you may have been given in the past. The reason a light breathing style is recommended is that deep breathing too easily turns into hyperventilation and makes anxiety worse. Breathe through your nose if it is comfortable to do so; this helps to ensure that you don't take really deep breaths. Aim to take breaths so light that it feels as if the air is just drifting into your nose.

Ideally, you will need a watch or clock that counts seconds to do the practice. Begin by taking a *small* breath in and holding it for six seconds. Just before breathing out again, think 'relax'; then breathe out. As you breathe out, try to feel a sense of releasing tension.

Next, breathe in for three seconds and out for three seconds. Try to breathe smoothly and lightly throughout the cycle. Continue this for the next minute. It will result in a breathing rate of ten breaths per minute—right in the middle of the normal, healthy range.

After ten breaths (one minute) take another small breath in, hold it for six seconds, think 'relax', and then breathe out while releasing tension.

Continue to repeat these steps until you have been through four or five cycles (about five minutes of practice). Initially, it may feel a little strange or unusual, but with practice most people find it very calming. In order to master this technique and have it become second nature to you, it is advisable to practise three or four times a day. You only need to spend five minutes at a time on it, so you really can't tell yourself you don't have the time for this one.

Commit yourself to practising the breathing control technique for five minutes at a time, four times a day. In between practices forget about your breathing—it will take care of itself. Don't let this become another focus of worry!

Troubleshooting

(P) 'I've tried relaxation and it doesn't work for me.'

(R) It typically takes two weeks of daily practice to see any measurable benefit. You owe it to yourself to persevere for at least this long to see if it can work for you.

(P) 'The relaxation practice makes me more anxious.'

(R) Some people experience this problem when they first begin to practise relaxation. It may have something to do with being more aware of anxieties when just sitting or lying still and not being distracted by other activities. My advice is to continue to practise the relaxation, at least for a two-week trial as noted above. Each day only go to the point where you begin to feel very anxious or uncomfortable and then leave it there for that day. Forget about it until your next practice, then again go only as far as is comfortable. This approach avoids turning your relaxation practice into another stressful event that you worry about in anticipation. Usually, it will gradually become more comfortable.

(P) 'The breathing control practice makes me feel like I need to take a big breath.'

(R) This is a common experience when first beginning to practise this technique. Try to persevere without stopping for the five minutes of the practice. Try to keep to the right timing. With continued practice this sense of needing to take a big breath will go away.

Long-term de-arousal strategies

There are many other activities that help to reduce arousal and stress levels. These include the many varieties of meditation, yoga and tai chi. If you are already engaged in these activities, keep up the good work. I regard them as helpful long-term strategies for controlling arousal and stress levels. There is some preliminary evidence that these activities reduce cortisol levels, which is desirable if these levels are heightened as a result of chronic anxiety.

If you are not currently practising any of these activities, however, I would advise that you first focus your time and energy on getting your anxiety and worry under control by using the strategies in this book. It's hard to learn too many things at once and even harder to find the time to practise several new skills. While yoga and meditation are likely to be helpful to you in the long term, they take some time to master and therefore some time to be beneficial. The progressive muscular relaxation and breathing control techniques, on the other hand, are quickly learned and soon show an effect. So start with these techniques and add yoga and/or meditation as part of your long-term maintenance plan.

PUTTING IN THE PRACTICE

There is no doubt that you will need to spend some time on the strategies outlined in this chapter. See this time as an investment in your future health. Chronic anxiety is no different from other types of long-term health problems such as diabetes or high blood pressure. If you had these problems you would also need to exercise regularly, and would also need to maintain a healthy weight and diet. View the de-arousal strategies as the foundation stone of your anxiety management program. We will build on this later by adding cognitive and behavioural strategies. A firm foundation of skills that enable you to rapidly reduce your level of anxiety and arousal will make it easier for you to effectively apply the cognitive strategies.

Keeping a record of the practice you do can help you stay motivated to keep these skills up. Each day record:

- exercise done
  - what you did
  - how far or how fast you went
  - how long you exercised for
  - general comments
- breathing control practices done
- relaxation practices done
- other de-arousal strategies employed (eg. yoga, meditation).

At this point, I suggest that you get yourself an exercise book. You can keep your records in it, and it will also be used later when we do some written practice of cognitive challenging and worry control techniques. Eventually, it will become your personalised record of anxiety and worry control strategies that work for you, and from which you can identify key components of your own anxiety control program to keep for future reference. When you get a bit stuck or have a setback it will remind you of what worked to help you feel better and therefore what you can do to reduce your anxiety once more.

Chapter Six

THE NATURE
OF WORRY

In order to gain more control over your anxiety and worry it is important to learn all you can about it. Most people feel their worry is uncontrollable. Many believe that it seems to come out of the blue or, alternatively, that it is constantly present. In fact, there are usually triggers, and the level of worry fluctuates, both over the course of the day and from day to day. You can learn more about your own pattern of worry and anxiety by keeping a diary or record of your worry episodes. This record is most helpful if it is structured, and pays attention to specific features, including:

- triggers to worry
- duration of worry episodes
- severity of worry episodes
- factors which help to stop a worry episode.

A template of a worry record is shown below. Fill out a worry record for each episode of worry that you have over the next two weeks. This will form a diary of your worry experiences and give you a good picture of your own worry pattern.

Worry record

Date: _____

Time worry episode started: _____

Time worry episode finished: _____

What was this worry about? _____

_____

_____

_____

_____

_____

What possibly triggered the worry?

(Ask yourself: What was I doing before the worry started?

What was I thinking about?

What did I just hear or read about?)

_____

_____

_____

_____

What did I do to try to stop the worry?

_____

_____

_____

_____

How did I stop worrying?

(Ask yourself: Did something distract me?

Did someone else do something that helped me to stop

worrying?)

_____

_____

_____

_____

How severe was this episode of worry?

0	1	2	3	4	5	6	7	8	9	10
nil			mild		moderate			severe		worst ever

What bothered me most about this worry episode?

_____

_____

_____

_____

Jenny was introduced to us on page 31. Below is a worry record from her diary.

Date: *Tuesday, 5th August*

Time worry episode started: *10.30 am*

Time worry episode finished: *3 pm*

What was this worry about?

> *I worried about my own symptoms and how difficult it can be to detect some things and how maybe it still could mean I have cancer.*

What possibly triggered the worry?

> *A friend called around and told me about her sister being diagnosed with multiple sclerosis. The doctors couldn't work out what was going on for a long time. I really didn't want to hear this story but I didn't know how to stop her telling me.*

What did I do to try to stop the worry?

> *I tried not to think about it. I checked how my head was feeling because I thought if it felt normal, I wouldn't worry, but then I couldn't tell if it was normal or not. I wanted to ring my GP but I was too embarrassed. I sat down and just tried to think it through and remind myself about all the things the specialists have told me, the normal test results, etc.*

How did I stop worrying?

> *I had to go and pick up the kids from school. When they got in the car they wanted to tell me all the exciting things that had happened and it distracted me from my worry.*

How severe was this episode of worry?

0	1	2	3	4	5	(6)	7	8	9	10
nil			mild		moderate			severe		worst ever

What bothered me most about this worry episode?

Worrying about having something really wrong is frightening. I also felt disappointed because I hadn't worried about this for a little while and thought maybe I was getting over it. I felt exhausted afterwards and it was hard to give energy to the kids.

YOUR OWN WORRY PATTERN

It's helpful to keep a record of your worry episodes for a week or two. If you only have occasional worry episodes, it might take a few weeks to collect a representative sample. On the other hand, if you suffer from almost constant episodes of worry, even a few days to a week will give you plenty of information for analysis. Ask yourself the following questions:

- Can I identify any patterns in the types of experiences or situations that trigger my worry episodes?
- Are there particular themes that recur in my worries? For example, money, ill health, mistakes, unhappiness, relationships.
- Are my worry episodes more or less severe than I thought?
- Do I have more or less time free of worry than I thought?
- Did I identify any strategies that effectively stop me worrying?
- What strategies do I currently use that *don't* help?

You will be asked to refer back to your worry diary to help you to analyse your own pattern of worry in more detail and plan appropriate treatment strategies. The rest of this chapter will attempt to give you a greater understanding of the forms worry can take and some of the common triggers.

WHAT-IF-ITIS

First of all, let's think about why we worry in the first place. What triggers worry? To answer this, have a look at your diary of worry records. You may have noticed some recurrent themes, such as money concerns, job pressures or uncertainty, relationship problems, or health anxieties. Are any of these worries about things that have already happened (eg. you can't pay a bill, you have just been told you are being retrenched at work, you have become ill, a relationship has broken up)? If so, are your worries about *what might happen next* or the problems that these events *might* lead to? If nothing bad has actually happened, are your worries about the *possibility* that something bad might happen in these areas?

Uncertainty has been shown to be a major trigger for worry. Does this fit your pattern? Often, worries will begin with, 'What if …':

- What if we get hit with an unexpected bill and can't pay it?
- What if this pounding heart is really a serious heart condition?
- What if my husband/wife gets fed up with all my anxiety and wants to leave?
- What if I make a mistake at work and lose my job?
- What if all this worry sends me crazy?
- What if I never get better?

What-if-itis is the most common type of worry in GAD, but sometimes might be disguised in another form. For example, the real fear behind 'Will I ever get over this?' is actually 'What if I never get over this?' 'Maybe' can also be closely related to 'what if …': 'My husband is late home … maybe he has had an accident.' You can see that 'what if …' could easily be substituted for the 'maybe' here.

Novelty or change can also trigger worry for some individuals, as these too inevitably involve some uncertainty. A change in routine, a new job, moving house, having to travel somewhere or take an unfamiliar route—these are just some examples.

CHARACTERISTICS OF WORRY

'Rumination'—a term used to describe the turning over and over of the same thoughts in one's mind—comes from the process used by animals such as cows and sheep to digest grasses. Grass contains a large proportion of tough fibre, which is difficult to break down and digest. If a human were to eat it, grass would pass through the body relatively unchanged (don't try this at home!). Cows and sheep have solved this problem by turning grass-like material over and over and over in their stomachs until it eventually breaks down. While the cow obtains benefit from this in the form of nutrition, a human ruminating about their problems tends to achieve little. Instead, they are often left feeling exhausted, demoralised and anxious. Rumination is a very unpleasant aspect of worry and can also make it hard to concentrate on anything else.

Most people feel as though their worry is uncontrollable. Worrying thoughts come into their mind at all times of the day or night, no matter how hard they try not to think them. Feeling unable to control your thoughts can be frightening. It also contributes to feeling somehow weak and generally out of control. Many people fear they are going crazy. They're not.

For most people, worry tends to be focused on the future: what might or could happen, what could go wrong. A study by Michel Dugas, Robert Ladouceur and colleagues in 1998 showed that sufferers of GAD are much more likely to worry about remote future possibilities than people without GAD. However, some sufferers worry most about threats they perceive in the present and a few seem fixed on the past. They regret past actions, thinking over and over 'if only ...' 'If only I had said/done ...' 'If only it hadn't happened.' 'If only she had said/done ...'

The good news is that all these patterns of worry can be overcome.

Is worry normal?

Research has shown that everyone worries. The main differences between excessive worry and normal worry are:

- People who worry about things to a normal degree generally feel able to control their anxiety. They can turn it off at will. Excessive worriers experience their worry as uncontrollable.
- People who worry to a normal degree see their worry as understandable and not excessive, in contrast to people who have GAD.
- Excessive worriers report more negative thoughts than people who have normal levels of worry.
- Excessive worriers worry more about events that are far in the future.

There is also some evidence for the saying that excessive worriers 'will find something to worry about'. A study by Graham Davey and Suzannah Levy, published in 1998, found a tendency for excessive worriers to even worry about things that were considered pleasant by others.

THE BENEFITS OF WORRY

It might surprise you to learn that worry has some benefits. However, I believe that these benefits are well outweighed by the negative aspects of worry, and I'm sure you'll agree. Logically, you wouldn't worry if it didn't seem, at some level, to be helpful. It's like being in a difficult relationship: it's easy to leave if it's all bad, but in real life most relationships have good and bad aspects. It's hard to leave and give up the good parts.

So how can worry possibly be helpful? To answer this, think about why you might have started worrying in the first place. Obviously, you were faced with some uncertainty in your life, which made you anxious. Anxiety is such an unpleasant feeling that we experience a strong urge to do whatever it takes to reduce it. If it is an anxiety-provoking situation, you escape from it. But what do you do when it is the thought that something might happen in the future that scares you? Or the fear that maybe something is terribly wrong at this very moment? Note the words 'might' and 'maybe'. In other words, there is considerable uncertainty. How does a person cope with anxiety from this type of trigger? One common response is to worry. It's not the best response, but it may be the best that an individual can come up with at the time, particularly if they're not aware of other coping strategies that might work better.

When we worry:

- We turn the concern over and over in our mind (rumination).
- We consider all the possible outcomes.
- We consider options for dealing with the various outcomes.

How might this be helpful? I would like you to take a minute to think about this question very carefully and see if you can think how worry might actually reduce your anxiety a little or otherwise seem to help. Write your answers here:

_____

_____

_____

_____

_____

These are some of the benefits of worry that other sufferers have identified over the years:

- When I worry, I feel as if I am 'covering all the bases'—that nothing will be able to take me by surprise.
- I would rather be prepared for the worst than have it take me by surprise.
- I believe I would cope better if the worst happened if I've thought about it first.
- If I think about it enough I can be sure I have done the best I can.
- If I worry about it enough I am more likely to find the solution to my problem.
- Worry makes me feel at least I am trying to do something about it (my problem or fear).
- If something bad happened and I hadn't worried about the problem I would feel guilty.

Do any of these perceived benefits apply to you? Perhaps worry seems to help by making you feel a little more in control—you feel as if you are doing something about the problem.

Magical thinking

Some of the beliefs about how worry helps fall into the realm of what psychiatrists call 'magical thinking'. This is the kind of thinking that underlies superstitions. It is also common and quite normal during childhood, and in dreams (when all sorts of completely impossible things happen). Thinking that you will only win the football game or pass your exam if you wear your 'lucky socks' is magical thinking. 'Don't step on the cracks' and 'don't break a mirror or you'll get seven years bad luck' are further examples of magical thinking. The saying about breaking mirrors is an interesting example. If the reasoning behind not breaking a mirror were that you might cut yourself, it wouldn't be magical. It's the fact that the belief isn't logical or realistic that makes it magical. However, these kinds of magical thinking are usually pretty harmless. They only become a problem if, for example, you can't find your lucky socks before a big football match and suffer an emotional collapse as a result!

Many anxious people use magical thinking without realising it. Some types of rituals in obsessive compulsive disorder (OCD) represent magical thinking. For example, feeling a need to repeat things that are said or thought in order to prevent harm. It is also common with OCD and GAD for sufferers to believe that simply having had a particular thought means it might come true. They reason, 'Why would I have even had that thought is there weren't some basis to it?' This is faulty reasoning. I might think about what it would be like to be the Queen of England, but that doesn't mean I belong on the throne.

Can you make things happen just by thinking about them? You have probably heard two statements that would seem to suggest this is true:

- the 'self-fulfilling prophecy' claim (if you worry too much about something negative happening you will bring it on yourself), and
- the notion that if you want something you need to see yourself achieving it.

Both these notions are unrealistic distortions of some sensible and factual concepts. Firstly, if you worry too much about something the net result could be that your fear comes true, or appears to come true. But this would not be simply because you thought about it too much. It would be because you changed your behaviour in response to the thought. For example, if I am worried that I will fail an exam, I might begin to spend my time worrying more and studying less. I might begin to sleep badly and lose concentration. I may fail my exam. However, it would not be as a direct consequence of having had thoughts that I could fail; it would be because I changed my behaviour (stopped studying) and allowed myself to ruminate about my worries, thereby raising my anxiety levels and making it harder to sleep and to concentrate. How many times have you had the thought, 'I might fail' and *not* failed?

Another example is seen in social phobia. Sufferers worry, with no evidence one way or the other, that someone doesn't like them. Because of this belief they may avoid the other person, and end up not talking to them. They then conclude, 'He didn't talk to me—that proves he doesn't like me.'

Humans seem naturally prone to this sort of thinking, but worriers seem especially affected. Too much magical thinking can contribute to excessive anxiety. And when you are making decisions about what action to take, relying on this style of faulty thinking can cause problems. Be alert for it in your own thinking.

If you believe that simply having a certain thought or idea about something—without any other action—can make it happen, you are thinking in a magical way. Some examples of magical beliefs about worry include the following:

- If I worry about it nothing bad will happen.
- If I don't worry something bad may happen and it will be my fault.
- I wouldn't have had the worry in the first place if there wasn't something wrong.

This is very different from positive thinking, where we visualise goals and encourage ourselves to achieve them. I'm all in favour of the kind of self-talk where we say, 'I can do that' to encourage ourselves. Mind you, even then, just saying it is not enough. We have to take action to make it happen. We have to learn new skills, practise them and try them out in real life situations.

It is important to point out that many of the people I have treated for excessive worry have been smart, sensible, functional individuals. They were not aware that they had been engaging in magical thinking, and were quite surprised to discover it! One young professional woman came to me to learn how to control her worry. I wanted to know whether she had in fact experienced many genuinely bad events in her life that might have contributed to her anxiety. She looked at me in an odd way, hesitated, then said rather sheepishly, 'No, but I think that maybe that is because I have worried so much.' She was only just realising that she believed her worry worked like a lucky charm to prevent bad things from happening. Now, you need to ask yourself: is this really likely to be true? Can you really prevent something bad from happening just by thinking it? Can you make it sunny and warm tomorrow just by thinking it? I think not!

Verbal versus visual

Researchers such as Thomas Borkovec and colleagues have identified a further benefit of worry. It distracts the sufferer from potentially even more terrifying *mental images* of disaster. Worry is predominantly a *verbal* strategy—it is a kind of anxious self-talk. This has been shown to be less anxiety provoking than mental images. It may explain why enabling individuals suffering from post-traumatic stress disorder to talk about their experiences can be helpful. One of the most distressing aspects of post-traumatic stress disorder is the repeated experience of mental images of the trauma. These may occur many times a day and are outside the sufferer's ability to control. It is known that many individuals who suffer from excessive worry also experience mental images of feared outcomes.

It is essential to acknowledge the apparent benefits that worry may have for you, even if these have up to now been subconscious. Most people are well aware of the negative aspects of too much worry, and wish to break the habit. However, if you believe subconsciously that worry is helping in some way, then you may actually feel *more* anxious initially if you reduce or stop your worrying. It may seem that, by not worrying, you are just going to sit back and let bad things happen. You may feel as if you are not taking control of the situation. Of course this is not really the case, as a more rational examination will show. But it can feel that way at first.

There is also a tendency to view anxiety as some sort of proof that something must be wrong. This is an example of what we call 'emotional reasoning'—using the existence of an emotion as proof that a particular event must have occurred—and will be discussed in more detail when we look at cognitive challenging.

If you are prepared for these reactions you can avoid falling into the trap of misinterpreting your anxiety. You will know that it is not evidence that you are doing the wrong thing by not worrying, or that things are going wrong.

HOW EFFECTIVE IS WORRY AT REDUCING YOUR ANXIETY?

As we've discussed, worry has some short-term anxiety-reducing benefits as it helps you to feel a bit more in control. But how much does your anxiety *really* reduce? You can probably answer this already. You could also consult your diary. The most likely response is 'not much'; you wouldn't be reading this book if you felt all that worry was just fine. It is important to be quite clear about this, to help you stay aware of your motivation to change.

Ask yourself the following questions (you may need to observe your own patterns of worry again over a few days in order to be able to answer them):

- Does my anxiety about a particular concern reduce when I worry?
- If so, for how long does it help?
- Does the worry go away, or does it just come back later?

Next, I would like you to consider what the *negative effects* of worry are for you. What problems does excessive worry cause you? List these below.

_____

_____

_____

_____

_____

Compare these to the positive benefits.

Once you have weighed the possible benefits of worry against its negative effects, it should be clear that the balance sheet is very much in favour of finding alternative strategies for dealing with problems and uncertainty rather than becoming anxious and worried. These strategies will be covered in the following chapters.

Chapter Seven

IT'S ALL ABOUT PROBABILITY

One of the fundamental problems in excessive worry and GAD is the tendency to overestimate the probability of a negative outcome, while underestimating the probability of a positive outcome. A *possibility* is soon viewed as a *probability*. A typical example of this is described below.

Kim's story

Kim, 40, worried whenever her teenage children were out with friends and not at home or school. She worried about them getting sick, being kidnapped, having accidents. She could not stop worrying until they returned home. They knew they had to call her as soon as they arrived where they were going, to reassure her they were safe. Kim would call them frequently while they were out to make sure they were okay. Her children knew how much she worried and so left their mobile phones on whenever possible. If she could not speak to them directly she would become extremely anxious and agitated. A typical chain of thought for Kim would be: 'Dinh should have arrived at the cinema by now ... why hasn't he called? Maybe he has had an accident ... he must be seriously injured or he would have called me ... I had better call the hospitals.' She would also not go to sleep at night until the children were all safely home.

Kim also worried about her husband's welfare. He knew to call her if he was going to be late home, or if he had to go out of the office for some reason, as Kim would become distraught if she tried to reach him and he was not in the office—especially if his colleagues did not know where he was.

Kim's behaviour was upsetting to her family and did not help her to worry any less.

This case study illustrates a number of bad habits that people who worry too much often develop over the years:

- jumping to conclusions
- overestimating probabilities
- catastrophising.

Another good example of catastrophising comes from Sam.

Sam

Sam, 45, had a long history of excessive worry, that tended to fluctuate in response to stress in his life. He found it hard to relax and had chronic insomnia. Recently, he had been working on a project that required considerable research. Sam was due to present his findings at a meeting that was to be attended by his boss and other colleagues from his department. He became extremely worried about his presentation, especially about his boss's reaction. Sam thought to himself: 'What if I have missed something important? My boss will think I'm incompetent … He probably knows all the information already … He'll think I'm useless and he won't want to renew my contract … I won't be able to find another job in this economic climate … We'll have to live off our savings and we'll never be able to afford to buy a house.'

Sam's thinking shows what we call 'the chain of catastrophe'. In this thought pattern, worriers start with one—usually unlikely—possibility of something going wrong and in their mind readily see this leading to a series of other bad outcomes. Like dominoes falling, their thoughts continue on, out of control, until a catastrophe is seen as the final outcome.

CAN YOU COPE?

Worriers also tend to underestimate their ability to cope with a bad outcome. Remember Matt, who became convinced he had failed his exam? Matt believed he could never live down the humiliation of failing. While it was very unlikely that he had actually failed, it was also unlikely that he wouldn't have coped if he did. It would have been disappointing, and it might have shaken his confidence, but it would not have been the unbearable catastrophe he had told himself it would be.

There is a formula for anxiety that goes like this:

$$\text{Anxiety} = \frac{\text{Probability} \times \text{Cost}}{\text{Ability to cope}}$$

In other words, if you believe that it is very likely that a feared outcome will happen, that it would be absolutely awful if it did, and that it would be unbearable for you and that you wouldn't cope, then you will experience a huge level of anxiety. On the other hand, if you think something is unlikely to happen, that it wouldn't be too bad if it did, and that you could quite easily cope, then you wouldn't feel too anxious at all.

Let's look at some hypothetical examples. Imagine that your birthday is coming up. In our first scenario your friends have suggested you all visit a local forest where a treetop walk has recently opened. You've seen pictures of it. It looks fairly solid—although you can see the ground through the slats of the boardwalk, and it is a long way up—and it has a balustrade. Despite feeling a bit nervous about heights you conclude that it seems pretty safe and you decide to go. On the day, you're a bit nervous but able to overcome it fairly easily.

In an alternative scenario, imagine that your friends have suggested you all go skydiving for your birthday, something none of you has ever done before. Suddenly, your mind is flooded with images of falling to the ground and injuring yourself. Despite knowing that an experienced instructor will be tandem diving with you, you feel that the risks are just too high. What if the parachute doesn't open? You've heard of people getting injured even with an instructor. You've heard of people getting killed! What if that was you? Or what if you got a head injury or terrible fractures? You couldn't cope with that. Now your anxiety level is very high. On the other hand, one of your friends may well be thinking, 'I've always wanted to try skydiving. This school must be very safe or they wouldn't still be in business. I bet it will feel incredible.'

Your level of anxiety is much higher than your friend's because you have assessed the situation quite differently. You see a high probability of serious harm. They see little chance of harm and haven't even considered how serious the consequences might be if something did go wrong—instead they are focused on the enjoyment they anticipate.

In this example, you have overestimated the likelihood of harm, but what about your friend's reaction? Interestingly, some people would say that your friend has assessed the risk of harm correctly; while others would argue that he has somewhat underestimated it. Opinions would differ because everyone has their own comfort level about taking risks. Financial planners are well aware of this. They often give their clients questionnaires designed to identify the level of financial risk with which the client will be comfortable. Investments with a potentially high yield tend to have a correspondingly higher risk of losing the investor money! Some people will view a one-in-a-thousand risk as negligible, while others will see it as unacceptably high. The assessment of risk will also be influenced by the nature and degree of the potential loss or harmful outcome. For example, if you go to the races and bet $5 on a horse, you'll be a lot less anxious about the outcome than if you have bet your house, irrespective of the horse's actual chance of winning.

A real life illustration of this principle comes from Craig Nelson, in his book *Let's Get Lost*, a humorous and entertaining account of his travels. For one trip he joins his brother and father on a restored nineteenth-century sailing ship, where they will act as part of the crew. One day it is his turn to help unfurl the sails. This requires him to climb up and all the way out to the end of the main spar, high above the ship, where he is tossed about in the rigging due to the windy conditions. Although he is in a safety harness, he is not reassured:

> … my major phobia is: *Manufacturer's Error*. When they say, 'We make these bolts to a tolerance of 400 000,' they mean that one of every 400 000 bolts fails. I'm convinced that's the bolt I'm going to get. Every time I think, 'Skydiving sure looks like a lot of fun!' it only takes a few seconds to remember that I'm bound to get the 1 in 500 000 parachutes that doesn't work. So there I was, high above the ship, teetering on a little rope, blinded by my own jacket, the wind and everyone else making me bounce up and down and swing back and forth, and all I could think was: *Manufacturer's Error*.

In order to reduce excessive worry, you will need to train yourself to make more realistic estimates of the actual probability of harm, and more realistic assessments of the real degree of threat. You also need to acknowledge your own strengths and ability to cope. Many worriers are highly critical of themselves. They think of themselves as weak because they easily become anxious and worry a lot. Nothing could be farther from the truth! In fact, to be able to carry on with daily life in the face of all that anxiety and worry requires a great deal of strength. Many excessive worriers still work or study, and many also manage a household and raise children. That really takes strength when you're constantly tired and plagued by worries. Take a moment, and think about how you've coped when things really have gone wrong.

Coping: what it really means

Many people have entirely the wrong idea about what coping means. They tell themselves that it means always being cool, calm and collected, no matter what the situation. They tell themselves that it means dealing with everything that life throws at them without a moment's anxiety. Without hesitating. Without raising a sweat. Making decisions and fixing things ... effortlessly.

Sorry, but that's complete rubbish! Coping just means that you get through. Most, if not all, people feel stressed when faced with a difficult problem or dilemma. They may find it hard to make an important decision, feel anxious when faced with the threat of illness, and challenged by difficult behaviour in colleagues or loved ones. They become distressed by relationship break-ups and job losses. They get tired, irritable and impatient when they're not getting much sleep or the children are seriously misbehaving. If they still go to work, manage the house and look after the children, then they're stressed, but coping.

The same applies to you. Sure, maybe you feel stressed and anxious by less serious or likely threats than the average person, but that doesn't mean you're not coping. Be a little kinder and fairer to yourself in your self-talk. A little encouragement is much more helpful than any amount of criticism.

Some people are lucky, or perhaps just young, and haven't had to deal with any serious losses, problems or threats in their life. In their case, the worry about what *might* happen has almost certainly been much more of a burden than anything that has *actually* happened. Think about what a waste this worry has been—when they could have been enjoying their good fortune.

Other people will have been through some significant trouble in their life. If this applies to you, look back on how you coped. Did you manage to keep going somehow? Was it as difficult to get through as you anticipated? How did you do it? If you did it then, you can probably do it again. A man who saw me for treatment of his excessive anxiety, and who developed and survived cancer during this time, later said to me, 'You know, it showed me that I can cope with the worst. I'm not so afraid of bad things happening any more because I think, "Yes, it will be bad, but I'll cope."'

Actually there is some fascinating new research looking at how people anticipate both positive and negative events in their lives, and how they subsequently cope with these events. So far these researchers, such as Timothy Wilson and Daniel Gilbert and colleagues, have not looked at worriers in particular, but just people in general. They have discovered that we humans tend to overestimate how much we will be affected by an event and how long the effect will last. When really good things happen, they are not as life changing as we anticipate they will be, and the happiness these events bring seems to fade back to normal everyday levels after a time.

Perhaps more relevant for worriers, however, are the findings about bad things happening. Humans predict that certain catastrophes will have a devastating effect from which they may never recover. In practice, this doesn't seem to eventuate. Certainly there is immediate and short-term distress, which can be intense. However, the distress is often not as great as would have been predicted, nor does it seem to persist. It seems that we are more resilient and cope better than we give ourselves credit for.

If you haven't always coped

A very small number of individuals may have been so overcome by their anxiety or depression in the past that they have had a period when they couldn't function, and needed time off work or even a hospital admission. Don't extrapolate from this to the future. It may never happen again. You can greatly reduce your risk of becoming so unwell again in the future by obtaining appropriate treatment. Both antidepressants (if taken on an ongoing basis) and cognitive behaviour therapy have been shown to reduce the risk of relapse. I tell my patients, 'Focus on the present and the future will look after itself.' In other words, dealing effectively with the problems and challenges of today is a good foundation for the future. No matter how hard you work at it, you simply cannot predict what will happen in the future with much accuracy, and you can waste a lot of time and energy trying. Wouldn't it be better to direct that energy to enjoying yourself and being productive in the present? That's not to suggest that you totally ignore the future. Rather, I suggest that you only think about the future in ways that are productive for you. If you can take a 'stitch in time', then do so. If you can take action that will have some future benefit (like investing money), then do so. The only thing I'm asking you *not* to do is ruminate about the future in an ineffective or unhelpful way.

Nervous breakdown

A few people become so anxious or depressed at some time in their life that they may suffer a 'nervous breakdown'. This is not a technical term. It has no precise meaning. The most accurate interpretation is to have become unable to function. If a person suffers such severe symptoms of anxiety, depression or psychosis* that they are unable to continue working, or look after themselves or others properly at home, then this probably constitutes a nervous breakdown. It usually requires hospital admission. However, just because you may be feeling very stressed, or anxious, or have become depressed does not mean you are suffering from a nervous breakdown. It also doesn't mean that a nervous breakdown is just around the corner. Every year more than *two million* Australians suffer from anxiety or depression severe enough to be considered a disorder, but very, very few of these end up in hospital.

* 'Psychosis' refers to symptoms such as delusions (strongly held, unusual and sometimes bizarre beliefs for which there is no logical evidence) and hallucinations (seeing things or hearing voices that are not really there). These are most commonly seen in illnesses such as schizophrenia and bipolar affective disorder. They can also be induced by some illicit drugs.

In the next chapter you will find a blueprint for controlling your excessive worry. You will also apply what you have learned so far, and discover further skills to learn and master. In the meantime, remember to keep practising your de-arousal strategies.

Chapter Eight

INTRODUCING THE WORRY CONTROL BLUEPRINT

You have learned much about the nature of worry, and have also learned about your own pattern of worry. You know the problems caused by being unable to tolerate uncertainty, and you know to expect that *not* worrying may increase your anxiety in the short term. So how are you supposed to deal with uncertainty? How can you respond to potential problems?

As you now realise, most worry episodes start with anxious thoughts, typically of the 'what if …' variety. These thoughts may have been triggered by a variety of situations, images or even other thoughts. Typically, once a thought occurs, the sufferer beings to ruminate about it. Hence, the anxious cascade. For example, 'My boss said he wants to see me later. Oh no! What if I've done something wrong? What could it be? Maybe he wasn't happy with that proposal I finished. Maybe it's because I went home early last week when my son was ill … even though he's usually very understanding. What if he's asking me in there to fire me? How would I cope? Maybe I should think of what I can say to him … What if I get so upset I can't even talk?' and so on and on and on!

Although your worrying up to now may have felt uncontrollable, you can in fact have a lot more control than you realise. It's just a matter of learning how to take control of your thoughts.

CONTROLLING YOUR THOUGHTS

There are two types of thoughts. The first type often just pops into your head; thoughts like, 'What shall I have for lunch?', 'That's a nice dress', and 'I wish I had a car like that!' But worries can also arise, such as, 'What if I get sick?' You can't control these types of thought—they just come into your head. What you *can* control, however, is how you choose to respond to them. This is the second type of thought. Let me illustrate this. Imagine that you are seated on a plane that is taxiing down the runway, about to take you off on a long awaited holiday. Suddenly, a thought pops into your head: 'What if the plane crashes?' At this point, you have two options. You could respond to this thought by actively thinking about it: 'Hmm, does the engine noise sound completely normal? What if there is a terrorist on board? People have been able to smuggle weapons on in spite of the security checks ... they're not very good anyway, everyone knows that. (You look around.) What about that man over there? He looks quite nervous and fidgety. What if he's really a terrorist? (The plane turns slightly.) Oh no! What was that? Why did we do that? What if we're already in trouble? Oh, this is terrible. I wish I'd never decided to go away.' Alternatively, you could choose to respond by saying, 'Well, that's really not very likely', and then look out the window, converse with your neighbour or start reading a book.

In the first instance you actively engaged with the thought that popped into your head. In the second you chose not to respond. Instead, you made a brief, sensible response to it and then changed the subject. View the thought that pops into your mind as a partner asking you to dance. You can accept and get up and dance, or you can politely decline. In the case of managing your worry you are better off not dancing!

It's virtually impossible to stop the worries by actively *trying to stop* them. To illustrate this point, try *not* to imagine a blue elephant dancing in a pink tutu and holding a little yellow umbrella ... Research has shown that the more we try not to think of something, the more frequently and persistently we experience the thought! I know that you would like to worry less, but attempting to reduce worries by trying not to think about them isn't going to work. You will only reduce the frequency and persistency of your worries by controlling how you respond to them in the first place. Let me explain how this works.

The blackmailer

Worries are like blackmailers. Hopefully you have no personal experience of this, but we all know how it works. A person has a terrible secret that the blackmailer finds out about. He contacts them and demands money for his silence, 'or else ...'. Terrified that the secret will get out, the victim pays up. What happens next? Do victim and blackmailer both live happily ever after? Unfortunately, not. There may be a brief respite but, as we all know, once the blackmailer realises that he can successfully intimidate the victim into paying, he comes back again and again. The victim suffers over and over. However, if one day the victim was to say to the blackmailer, 'That's it. I've had enough. Go ahead and tell whoever you want, I'll live with it', then the blackmailer would instantly lose his power over his former victim.

Now imagine your worries as blackmail. You feel the urge to 'pay' the blackmailer by ruminating about your fear, worrying about it over and over in your head, trying to find a solution. It seems as if you'll feel better if you do this. (We discussed the hidden benefits of worry in chapter six.) Maybe the worry goes away for a while. Sometimes it goes away for a short time, sometimes longer, but the problem is that it always comes back. Worrying about it hasn't solved anything; it has just locked you into repeating the same pattern over and over again.

The key to managing your worry is to confront your fears and deal with them effectively, without reinforcing them. By starving your worries of reinforcement—by not paying the blackmailers—they will eventually get weaker and might even go away and leave you alone. This model for controlling your anxiety is outlined below. I have called it the Worry Control Blueprint.

DEALING WITH WORRY—STEP BY STEP

Let's work through the Worry Control Blueprint one step at a time. The process starts when you get a worry. This is represented in the first box as 'what if ...'. If you tend to experience worries that sound more like 'how will I ...', 'if only ...', or some other phrase typical of your pattern of worry, write this down in the box to remind yourself what to listen out for in your head.

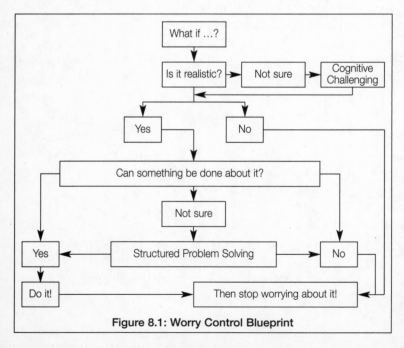

Figure 8.1: Worry Control Blueprint

Follow the flow chart and you will see that the first question to ask yourself about your worry is, 'Is it realistic?' Some worries will be obviously unrealistic, some will be realistic, and in other cases you may have worried yourself into such a state that you can't be sure any more. Let's look at some examples of the various types.

Example 1

Worry: 'What if the bank forecloses on our mortgage because our payment was a week late?'
Question: Is this a realistic fear?
Answer: 'No! It has happened before and they don't even make contact with us.'
Blueprint says: Then stop worrying about it!

Example 2

Worry: 'What if our house is burgled while we're away on holiday?'
Question: Is this a realistic fear?
Answer: 'Yes, it happens.'
Blueprint says: Can something be done about it?

Example 3

Worry: 'What if I'm on completely the wrong track with my assignment and I'm wasting valuable time?'
Question: Is this a realistic concern?
Answer: 'Not sure.'
Blueprint says: Apply cognitive challenging.

It is important to note that I am not suggesting that you ignore problems. You can see from the blueprint that if you are facing a realistic problem, the recommendation is to apply a structured approach to attempting to solve the problem. This is quite different to either ignoring it or worrying about it in an anxiety provoking but ineffective way.

New skills

To use the Worry Control Blueprint effectively you will need to master three skills. These are:

1. cognitive challenging
2. structured problem solving
3. 'stop worrying about it' (not the same as 'don't think about it').

Cognitive challenging helps you to put your fears in perspective. It encourages you to make realistic estimates of the probability of a feared outcome, and to keep a realistic perspective on how bad a feared outcome might really be if it were to happen. Structured problem solving is a strategy that can be employed to help answer the question 'Can something be done about it?' As its name implies, it is a structured approach to looking for potential solutions to actual problems that you are facing, and which may be triggering your worry. It can also be helpful when a person is faced with a difficult, and therefore worrying, decision to make, as in Stan's case (see page 39).

At each stage of the blueprint, one of three options may apply: 'yes', 'no' or 'not sure'. If you can answer a definite 'yes' or 'no' to the questions about whether your worry is realistic and whether something can be done about it, you move to the next step. I suggest deciding whether your fear or worry is realistic as the first step, because there is really no point in wasting your time on a worry that is unrealistic in the first place! Hence, if you can see right away that your worry is unrealistic, the Worry Control Blueprint takes you straight to 'Then stop worrying about it!' This is a skill in itself, and undoubtedly the most difficult to learn, but all it takes is practice.

Whenever your response to the gatekeeper question is 'not sure', you are directed to use a strategy designed to help you decide whether the answer is 'yes' or 'no'. These strategies—cognitive challenging and structured problem solving—enable you to progress to the next level of worry management and will be discussed in detail in subsequent chapters.

Chapter Nine

STRUCTURED PROBLEM SOLVING

Structured problem solving, based on the work of Thomas D'Zurilla and others, is an effective way of making decisions and resolving problems. It is one of the techniques that research has repeatedly demonstrated to be helpful in reducing worry and anxiety. Despite this, structured problem solving is under-utilised, probably because at first glance it looks too simple to be very effective. Certainly the structure is straightforward. Don't let this deceive you into thinking it can't do much for you: it's a much more powerful technique than it might appear, and absolutely indispensable in controlling worry. It may take some practice but it's worth it. It will also take time. However, most of my patients find that they can work through a problem in 30 to 45 minutes. Contrast this with the hours you could spend worrying unproductively about a problem: you might worry for days on end and still be no nearer to making a decision or solving the problem. By comparison, an investment of 30 to 45 minutes looks good! I will be up front at the outset and admit that this technique can't do magic—sometimes there just won't be a solution to your problem. That's life. But there is great value in knowing this, as it means you can then choose to stop wasting your time worrying about a problem that can't be solved anyway. This is an important element of the Worry Control Blueprint.

Structured problem solving has six steps:

1. describe the problem
2. brainstorm
3. evaluate possible solutions
4. choose the best solution or combination of solutions
5. plan to implement the chosen solution/s
6. review the outcome.

Many readers will look at this list and say, 'Oh, yes. That's exactly what I do at work when there is a problem to be solved.' Yet very few of the individuals who have said this to me over the years have ever applied this technique in a disciplined way to their personal problems and decisions. Either it never occurred to them, or they saw their personal problems as being different in some way. However, structured problem solving is an effective technique for a wide range of problems, personal or professional.

STEP ONE: DESCRIBE THE PROBLEM

This is often more challenging than it appears, but it is crucial to the success of problem solving. For example, take the problem, 'I hate my job.' Where would you start with this problem? It's just too broad. Your first suggestion might be to say, 'get a new job', but it's hard to think of any alternatives. It would be better to try and really pin down the problem. The example below illustrates this clearly.

Heather's story

Heather worked as a clerk/typist in a firm of solicitors. She worked for a partner, although her immediate supervisor was the partner's executive secretary and personal assistant. She came to see me, complaining that she didn't like her job and didn't know what to do. I asked Heather whether it was the work she didn't like. She replied, 'Oh no. The work is quite interesting, actually.' So then I asked her if it was the physical environment of her office that was the problem. 'Oh, that's okay,' she said. I began to scratch my head. Is there a problem with your supervisor? 'Oh no, she's really nice,' Heather replied. Is there a problem with your boss, I asked her? 'We-ll …' she said, 'Sort of. I mean, he's quite nice, but he keeps giving me all this typing to do just before I'm supposed to finish.'

The problem for Heather was that she worked in the city but lived a long way out in a new suburban development. She had to catch a train and then a connecting bus. The bus service was infrequent, and if Heather missed her usual bus she had to wait 45 minutes for another. Given that it already took her one and a half hours to get to work, this became very burdensome for her. So, the problem was not actually 'I hate my job'—she didn't. Her real problem was: 'My boss has a habit of giving me a large typing job late in the day that makes me miss my connecting bus and I don't get home until very late.'

Let's look at another example. Stan's story was described on page 39. He can't decide whether or not to take a redundancy package that his workplace is offering. He worries about making the wrong decision. What is the real problem here? Stan thinks it's 'Should I take the redundancy package or not?' But that's not actually it. Stan's ultimate goal is to achieve financial security for himself and his wife in the future. Against this he is trying to balance his dissatisfaction with his current job. So Stan's problem really is: 'I don't like my job much but I need financial security for the future.' In this context, the redundancy package becomes just one option to consider, and not the problem itself.

STEP TWO: BRAINSTORM

This step is about trying to think laterally and generate as many potential solutions to your problem as possible. The term 'brainstorming' is used to remind you to think creatively and 'outside the square'—to really look for as many alternatives as you can. Most of us have a tendency to think along the same old lines and often turn to the same sorts of solutions we've tried before. There's nothing wrong with this but, to give ourselves the best chance of finding a good solution, we need to look more widely and have as many options as possible to consider.

Many of us are inclined, when pondering how to solve our problems, to think: 'Well, I could ... no that would never work', or 'Maybe I could ... no, I'd never be able to do that.' In other words, we may be excluding potential solutions prematurely, before really considering them. So in this step, it is recommended that you don't exclude *any* ideas that you have. It's fine to consider ideas that might seem implausible, silly or 'way out'. You never know when an idea might have more merit than initially thought, or when it might lead to other more practical ideas. In step three you will examine all your options very thoroughly, so don't be concerned that you might end up trying something strange or doomed to failure!

It can be helpful to ask friends or family for their ideas, if you're comfortable discussing your problem with them. You're not asking them to solve your problem, but they may think of an idea that you didn't. The more ideas the better. Again, even if their ideas don't sound like they would suit you, don't exclude them before giving them some thought.

As an exercise, try brainstorming potential solutions to Heather's problem with her boss and write your ideas down here.

Potential solutions:

_____

_____

_____

_____

_____

I have presented this example to patients and in my lectures to general practitioners and trainee psychiatrists over the years. Here are some of the suggestions they have made:

- get a new job
- move closer to the job
- buy a car
- talk to the boss
- email the boss
- write to the boss
- talk to the supervisor
- contact her union.

How many of these did you identify? Did you have any other ideas?

STEP THREE: EVALUATE POSSIBLE SOLUTIONS

In this step you will carefully scrutinise all the options you identified in step two. It is essential to be realistic and practical in your assessment. For example, would you have the time to implement the potential solution? Would you have the resources, both personal and financial? If we look at Heather's case, speaking directly to the boss might take courage and self-confidence. Not everyone would be able to do this. Moving house might cost too much money to be practical. Also ask yourself whether a potential solution would be likely to cause problems of its own. Would it completely resolve the problem or only be a partial solution?

In this step it's important to be thorough in your analysis. That means evaluating the pros and cons of *each* solution. These all need to be written down—you can't keep all this information in your head; you're not a computer and you simply don't have enough RAM! The other advantage of this is that if you get interrupted, or haven't time to complete it all in one session, you can easily come back to the exercise without losing any information or wasting your previous effort. It may seem time consuming but, as mentioned earlier, a structured problem solving exercise is commonly completed in about 45 minutes. Compare this with the time you could spend worrying unproductively about the same problem: many worriers could waste days without coming close to a solution.

In looking at the pros and cons of each possible solution it will probably occur to you that not all pros and cons are equal. Some advantages are very significant and others may be minor. Similarly, some disadvantages of a possible solution will be more serious than others. In order to take account of this, I have developed a rating system for my patients to use. To keep it simple, I suggest a three star rating system. One star (*) for a minor pro or a minor con— something that wouldn't influence you very much. Two stars (**) for a moderate pro or con. Three stars (***) for an important pro or serious con—something that would have a significant influence on your decision. The stars can also incorporate some measure of likelihood. For example, when Heather rates 'Same thing could happen in the new job' in her cons list for solution one (below), she gives it two stars. A new job would be just as bad as the current one if the same problem happened again, and on this basis the con perhaps deserves three stars. However, because Heather thinks the problem's not that likely to recur in a new job she chooses to give it only two stars.

Of course, you can use any rating system you wish. I just chose this one because it's simple to use and it jumps out at you from the page. A quick glance is often enough to show you the potential solutions that are looking good and those that have too many disadvantages or too few advantages to compare favourably with the others.

Let's now look at Heather's possible solutions and how she might have rated them.

Solution one: get a new job

Pros	Cons
Would solve the current problem.***	Same thing could happen at the new job. **
	Could be difficult to find a new job. **
	There might not be many jobs close to where I live. *
	Might not find a job with all the good aspects of the current job. ***

Solution two: move closer to the job

Pros	Cons
Wouldn't matter as much to get extra work late in the day (but I'd still rather finish on time). **	Might be expensive in this area. *
Generally less time travelling, and therefore more time to myself. ***	Would have to spend some time looking for a place. *
	I like where I'm living now. **

Solution three: buy a car

Pros	Cons
I'd love to have a car. ***	Nowhere to park it where I work. ***
	I can't afford a car. **

Solution four: talk to the boss

Pros	Cons
I could deal with him directly about the problem. **	I'm really anxious about talking to him about it. ***

Solution five: email the boss

Pros	Cons
Don't have to deal with him directly. ***	Would seem a bit rude. ***

Solution six: write to the boss

Pros	Cons
Don't have to deal with him directly. ***	Might seem a bit unusual. **
	He'd probably want to come and talk to me about it anyway. ***
	Not very direct. **

Solution seven: talk to my supervisor

Pros	Cons
Don't have to deal with the boss directly. ***	She might not explain things right. *
Nancy is very understanding. ***	
Nancy gets on very well with the boss and is likely to be effective. ***	

Solution eight: contact my union

Pros	Cons
Don't have to deal with the boss directly. ***	Might seem like I have a grievance, which I don't. ***
	Might take a long time to do anything. **
	It is better etiquette to try to solve the problem locally first. ***

Notice that the word 'might' occurs in some of Heather's statements. Your assessments will be more accurate if you can find out more information about any possible eventualities. After all, if it was *definitely* the case that Heather would not be able to afford to live in the area where she works, she might rate this factor more highly. Or if she discovered it wasn't as expensive as she thought, she would perhaps rate it lower or even delete it as a disadvantage. How can she get more information? She might choose to look through the To Let section in the newspaper, or contact some real estate agents or agencies that deal in share accommodation. Your assessments of risk and benefit will be most accurate when they are based on facts, so always try to get as much factual information as you can. In some cases, there may not be any source of factual information, and then you will need to try to be as realistic as you can in your assessment of the likelihood of that pro or con.

By trying to base your assessments on factual information wherever possible, you will know that you have taken into account all possible factors. This becomes important later when you work through the rest of the Worry Control Blueprint to the 'Then stop worrying about it!' step. It will be much easier to let go of a specific worry if you are convinced in your own mind that you considered the problem thoroughly and researched as much factual information as possible to guide and inform your decision.

Don't kid yourself

Be sure to be realistic when estimating how difficult a solution would be for you to carry out, or how much you would care about a particular pro or con. Trying to fool yourself into thinking something doesn't matter to you when it really does, won't work. You won't feel as though your problem solving conclusions can be relied on and you won't act on them. If you think you might be overreacting, that's another matter. In this instance, cognitive challenging might help you put the pro or con into a more realistic perspective (see chapters ten and eleven).

STEP FOUR: CHOOSE THE BEST SOLUTION OR COMBINATION OF SOLUTIONS.

Heather is now in a position to compare each of her possible solutions based on how she rated their pros and cons.

Solution	Pros	Cons
One	3	8
Two	5	4
Three	3	5
Four	2	3
Five	3	3
Six	3	7
Seven	9	1
Eight	3	8

It is immediately apparent that, for Heather, solution seven (talk to her supervisor) is the best choice. It not only has the highest points difference between pros and cons, but it also has the highest score for pros and the lowest score for cons. However, in working through this exercise Heather also noted that solution two (move closer to the job) was an attractive option and so decides it's something she might look into further in the future. It turns out that Heather will implement two solutions.

You may have rated the options that Heather identified differently. You may even have come up with some additional possibilities to consider. The point is that Heather thought of as many possible solutions as *she* could, and rated them in a way that was appropriate for *her*. So, while in step two you may have taken note of other people's suggestions, be sure that you rate them according to how *you* feel about them. If other people try to push you into using their suggestion, thank them for their concern but point out that it's important for you to make the decision that is best for you. What's right for others may not be what's right for you. Have some confidence in your ability to make decisions for yourself.

An element of risk

It's important to note that structured problem solving doesn't take all the worry out of making decisions. There is nothing on earth that can guarantee you things will turn out fine. In other words, there is still some uncertainty about what will happen in the future. This is part of life. We simply can't eliminate all uncertainty no matter how much we would like to do so. All that any of us can do is get as much information as we can to base our decision on, and consider our options carefully. Then we have to wait and see. Structured problem solving can help you make the best decision possible *with the information available to you at the time*. We could all make money on the share market or win Lotto if we knew a week ago what we know today—but we don't. So be fair to yourself. Make the best decision that you can, but don't expect yourself to be able to make the 'right' decision every time, since only time will tell. *No one* can do better than this!

Interestingly, most millionaires have both won and lost fortunes. In general, highly successful business people tolerate a much higher level of risk than the average person. They make careful assessments, but at the end of the day will invest more money in something they see as having a fair chance of success even though there is also a chance they could lose their money. You or I might not be comfortable investing unless we had some sort of guarantee that we would at least get back the money we'd invested. This greater tolerance for risk allows successful business people to take opportunities that may result in large profits, but also large losses. Business people that are less successful at identifying potentially profitable opportunities may sustain more losses or fail to make such large gains, and so generally don't come into prominence. Determine your own level of comfort with risk and take this into account when assessing pros and cons. Just remember that you can't eliminate *all* risk and uncertainty.

STEP FIVE: PLAN HOW TO IMPLEMENT YOUR CHOSEN SOLUTION/S

It's not the time for a well-deserved rest just yet. Many people fail to implement a potentially effective solution. It is important to make a practical, specific plan for implementing your chosen solution. This is exactly what you would do at work, yet many people don't follow through on planning when they make personal and domestic decisions.

Let's return to our example. Heather has chosen to speak to her immediate supervisor and also to look for a place closer to home. She needs to decide exactly how and when she will implement these decisions. What will she say and when will she say it? How and when will she approach the task of finding a new place to live?

Heather decides that the immediate priority is to try to get home earlier. She often has morning tea with her supervisor, so this could be an opportunity to talk to her—but usually other secretaries are around. However, she realises that she could use the opportunity to arrange a meeting with her supervisor for later in the day. She then thinks about exactly what she will say. As a general guideline to effective communication, try to use 'I' messages to explain how you feel about something, and be clear about what you would like to happen or how the other person could help. So, Heather might decide to say something like, 'I have a problem that several times each week I'm not getting home until after seven o'clock because Mr Smith is giving me some work at the last minute. I have to stay late to get it done and I miss my bus. I'm being paid for it, but getting home so late is getting me down. I need to be able to catch the 5.45 train at the latest in order to make my bus connection. That means I would need to leave the office by 5.30. I wonder if you would be able to help me with this problem?'

Heather is polite but very clear about both how the problem is affecting her and what she would like to happen. Note that she focuses directly on what would solve her problem (getting out of the office by 5.30). Heather decides that the very next day at work she will ask her supervisor for time to talk, at her convenience. When she has the meeting with her supervisor she will say what she planned (and practised) at home.

With respect to finding a place closer to home, there are more steps involved. As part of her research, Heather found out about rental prices. She decided that she could not really afford an apartment on her own close to work, but that she would be able to afford to share a place. Heather also thought that she would enjoy sharing with some other people her age, as up to now she had been living at home with her family. She realised that the first step for her would be to talk it over with her parents—she wasn't in a big hurry to move out and would prefer to have her parents' support for the idea. She decided to do this some time in the next six months. During this time she would save for her share of the bond and possibly keep her eye on prices and availability. Once she was ready to proceed, her plan would be to look through the newspaper each week and also check a useful Internet site that she had found. She would get advice from her parents and from friends about what to look for and possible traps to avoid.

STEP SIX: REVIEW THE OUTCOME

Structured problem solving has one more step, just as important as all the others: review the outcome of your chosen solution. Ideally, you decide when and how to review the outcome before you even implement the solution—it really is an integral part of the problem solving exercise. Your review strategy will vary with the solution. For Heather, who plans to talk to her supervisor the very next day, she might set an initial review for the next evening, looking at how her supervisor responded. If the supervisor responded by saying she would try to solve the problem for Heather, this would confirm that the chosen solution remains the best approach. She would then set a further review date for the near future, allowing what she thinks would be a reasonable timeframe for her supervisor to take action.

In another type of problem, a different review strategy might be appropriate.

Phil and Shanti's story

Phil and Shanti have been having problems with the behaviour of their five-year-old son: he's been biting his younger brother. They did a problem solving exercise and decided to obtain advice from a child psychologist, who recommended that they try a number of strategies. On the psychologist's advice they decided to use the strategies for the next two months and then review their progress. They need some way of deciding if the strategies are working, so the psychologist recommends that for two weeks before they start the strategies they keep a record of the number of times that Jack bites Nathan. This is easy because Nathan runs screaming to them or any caregiver every time it happens! This initial record will be the baseline. Phil and Shanti then need to commence using the strategies as well as continue to record instances of biting. They should expect to see a difference in Jack's behaviour within the two-month review time and their records mean they will have a clear basis on which to measure any improvement.

Sometimes a solution will require a one-off action plan, as in Heather's case. In other instances it will require a behavioural strategy to be implemented numerous times as in Phil and Shanti's case. In yet other cases the solution may be a cognitive strategy. For example, you may decide that you will tackle your excessive worry by trying to use the strategies in this book. You could set a timeframe in which to determine whether the book is helpful to you or not and could then measure your progress by using the Penn State Worry Questionnaire before you start, and then again after one or two months. Alternatively, you could record the number and severity of worry episodes or simply do a daily rating of your overall sense of wellbeing, before and after starting to implement the strategies.

Whatever the solution you decide to implement, your subsequent review of its effectiveness will reveal one of the following outcomes. Your problem will be:

- solved
- partially solved
- still with you but changed
- still with you and just the same.

If your problem is solved, great! For all the other possible outcomes, it's time to go through the structured problem solving exercise again, taking into account any new information or changes that have occurred. Try not to feel too disappointed—in real life many problems are not solved at the first try. Think about trying to get your renovation or building plans through Council, giving up smoking or looking for a new hobby. You might need to make several attempts at these things to succeed. In practice, people rarely find that their problem is still with them but utterly unchanged. However, if this should be the case, then particular attention to the brainstorming step could be most useful. If you have not already done so, it could be helpful to get some advice or suggestions from others. If there is more information available that might impact on your decision, it would be good to follow this up.

Troubleshooting

(P) 'What happens if I make my decision, but then find out some new information?'

(R) If you haven't yet implemented your decision, you can go through the steps again. The new information may allow you to consider new solutions that weren't available before. Or it may simply change some of your pros and cons or the weighting given to them. Go on to the next step as usual.

If you have already implemented your solution, then consider how the new information affects your evaluation of the solution you've implemented. Does it significantly change the likelihood that your chosen solution (or solutions) will be effective? If not, then there's no need to do anything. If you think it would reduce the effectiveness or appropriateness, then can you take additional action? Sometimes, new information will affect an outcome in a significant way. For example, you are about to move into your new home when plans are announced for your road to be turned into a major new freeway. You had checked with the planning department beforehand and there was no hint of this. Clearly, it would have affected your decision to buy the house, but it's too late now. So, rather than spend the rest of your life ruminating on 'if only …' — a very close cousin to 'what if …' — a better approach is to make your new situation the subject of a problem-solving exercise and look at your options. Don't 'shift the goal posts' on yourself and blame yourself for not having seen into the future. No one can make decisions that turn out for the best every time, because no one can see into the future.

(P) 'All the solutions look equal.'

(R) Sometimes this is just how it is. Relax, it means that it really doesn't matter that much which one you choose! Just be sure that you have been honest with yourself in your answers and have been as thorough as you can in identifying options and basing your assessments on fact whenever you can.

(P) 'I don't like the solution that comes out as the best one.'

(R) If this happens, look back on your pros and cons and the ratings you gave them. Have you been in touch with your real feelings about each option? Have you been honest with yourself? Look carefully to see whether you can think of any pros and cons for any of the possible solutions that you might have missed the first time. If there is someone with whom you are comfortable discussing your problem, ask them to look over your ratings. Sometimes people who know us well can see where we may have rated a pro or con in a way that doesn't seem to fit with what they know about our personality or usual way of thinking. In particular, look out for ratings that you have based on what you think you *should* feel or think, rather than on what you actually think. For example, if Phil and Shanti had thought, 'We should be able to handle this ourselves', they would not have rated the option of seeing a child psychologist very highly and might have prevented themselves from getting the sort of help that would effectively solve their problem.

(P) 'I can't find the perfect solution.'

(R) The structured problem solving technique helps you realise that there isn't any perfect solution to your problem or dilemma. There wasn't a single one of Heather's potential solutions that had no possible disadvantages. Many worriers turn problems around and around in their heads, ruminating about them for days, weeks or months because they believe the 'right' solution is out there somewhere. In their minds the 'right' solution means the 'perfect' solution. The perfect solution will solve their problem completely and have no downside. The perfect solution is a rare animal that is almost never seen in adult life. When you were a child, things were probably more black and white. The right decision was usually to obey the rules and do what your parents and teachers told you. Adult life is far more complex. It's not black and white. By far the majority of decisions are compromises.

If you have ever bought or rented a property you will know this already. Most people identify a number of attributes they are searching for in their next abode. For example, they might want a freestanding house, to have the living areas facing north, three bedrooms, two bathrooms, a separate dining room, a large garden, a dwelling close to public transport. They might want to avoid a main road. They will be trying to achieve all this on a certain budget. (My own personal motto has always been, 'I know what I want, I just can't afford it.')

Inevitably, there will have to be a compromise. You might find a place that has everything you want, except it's a semi-detached and the garden is small; or it's more of a walk to public transport than you'd hoped but has everything else. If it's close enough to what you want, if it has the most important attributes, you might compromise. Alternatively, you could keep looking. You'd need to balance the cost in terms of time and effort with the likelihood that you'll get closer to what you want. We make compromise decisions all the time—with jobs, cars, houses and holidays. In reality, almost every decision we make in adult life is a compromise. Therefore, the best decision—the 'right' decision— is the one that maximises advantages and minimises disadvantages.

Chapter Ten

IDENTIFYING YOUR COGNITIONS

The history and basic principles of cognitive behaviour therapy (CBT) were outlined in chapter four. Cognitive challenging is a technique central to CBT. In essence, it is about challenging yourself to consider an issue from other points of view. Its goal is for you to think about things in as helpful a way as possible. It is important to stress that it is not just 'positive thinking', particularly if this is equally as unrealistic as a negative point of view. For example, if you are about to sit an exam or go for a job interview, it is unhelpful and almost certainly unrealistic to be saying to yourself, 'Oh, why bother trying? I'm only going to fail anyway.' On the other hand, it is also unrealistic and unhelpful to say things like, 'It doesn't matter if I get the job or not. It doesn't worry me at all.' Cognitive challenging is about making realistic assessments of situations and problems. It is about trying to think helpfully but realistically about things. This is often referred to as 'realistic thinking' or 'straight thinking'. The first step in cognitive challenging is to learn how to identify your cognitions (thoughts).

THE BRAIN AS AN INFORMATION PROCESSOR

The brain is a highly sophisticated information processor. Night and day it is fed information from our senses. Even though we may be asleep, our ears still hear things, our nose still smells and our sense of touch continues to operate. While awake we also have visual and taste information to process. Scientists now suggest that perhaps one of the most important jobs the brain does is to process all this information and keep it in the background, *away from* our conscious attention. It is generally felt that we have a fairly limited capacity for actively paying attention to something. This is called our 'attentional capacity'. If we were to be constantly aware of every single smell, every sensation, every sound and sight, we would be so overwhelmed with information we could not think clearly. So, in fact, perhaps the biggest job the brain does is to quietly process this information and file it away or bring it to our attention, depending on its level of importance.

To illustrate this further, think about what is happening to you now. Perhaps you are sitting somewhere and concentrating on this book. However, if you consciously think about it, you may realise that simultaneously you had some awareness of background noises—perhaps of birds or traffic or people talking. You will be aware of the quality of the light, whether you are indoors, outdoors or near a window. You will know what the chair you are sitting on feels like and what the air temperature is. You may now notice whether there have been any smells in the background—perhaps someone is making coffee or wearing perfume near you.

In my office I am lucky enough to have a window that looks out on a garden. When I do this exercise with my patients, we realise that we can usually hear birds outside, and on warm days there are often children shouting in play from nearby houses. The chairs will have a particular feel and we will be aware of whether it is sunny or overcast outside. I don't have air conditioning so the inside temperature can also vary quite a bit.

Think about the information your brain has been processing. Importantly, be aware that this processing results in certain inferences being made and conclusions being drawn. For example, imagine that you now smell smoke. Your brain will automatically process the information about this new smell. You will instantly decide whether someone is having a barbecue, whether the toast is burning, or whether there is a house fire. If you decide a neighbour is having a barbecue you will just file this information away in the background. On the other hand, if your brain interpreted the likely cause of the smoke as potentially dangerous—such as toast burning or a building on fire—then you would be instantly alerted. This information would take precedence over your reading much like a news flash interrupts a television program. The flight or fight response might even be activated depending on how much of a threat your brain decided was present. If you thought someone was burning the toast you might feel slightly uneasy depending on who you thought was in the kitchen (for example, a child of six as opposed to a 17 year old would usually raise different levels of concern). If it smelled like a house fire you would be much more concerned, and if it seemed close enough to be *your* house you would probably jump up in alarm.

This processing of information, resulting in interpretations being made and conclusions being drawn, is happening night and day. You can see that when you interpret a situation as potentially dangerous, the flight or fight response is activated. You will also remember that this is an automatic process that can't be changed: if you feel threatened you will get anxious. So, how can we stop this occurring?

PROGRAMMING THE BRAIN

The answer lies in how we program the brain. Think about the example above. How would your brain decide what the likely source of the smoke was? It would depend a great deal on your previous experience. It is likely that you have been to a number of barbecues in your life, and so have developed a very good idea of what this type of smoke smells like. Similarly, you have probably burned your share of toast. On the other hand, you may have had no first hand experience of a house fire. However, you have probably come across the smoke from paper burning (for example, to start a fire in a fireplace) and from general rubbish. From this your brain might extrapolate and make an inference. In this case, you would have more likelihood of being wrong: you would have to rely more on assumptions because of your lack of first-hand experience. In this same way—through experience and inference—we program our brains about how to interpret a wide range of information that comes from our environment.

So far we have looked at fairly straightforward types of situations. Birds singing and barbecue smoke are reasonably simple. But what about situations where the information is new, very complex or confusing? In novel situations you may have little experience on which to draw; for example, encountering a particular problem for the first time in a new job or that anxious feeling you get when you think you may have accidentally deleted some important data. Social situations can also be very complex, as much of the information we receive can be vague and ambiguous. Is the interviewer frowning because he doesn't understand me, because he doesn't believe me, or because he is just concentrating hard on what I am saying? In these situations we may have less experience to draw on and less concrete information available to us. There is thus a much higher likelihood of drawing an inaccurate conclusion.

We also need to be aware that sometimes our prior experience can be misleading, too. For example, perhaps you have always thought that the birdsong you hear in your backyard is coming from a lorikeet. Perhaps someone once told you this. Now imagine that one day you visit a bird park where you can see and hear each type of bird sing and the sign on the cage tells you which bird is which. Suddenly, you realise that lorikeets really have a screeching call and that the pleasant whistling in your backyard was actually coming from a robin. Similarly, we can misinterpret certain sensory information because we do not know the real facts. A good example of this is the tendency for many anxious individuals to interpret feelings of unreality as evidence that they must be going crazy. The truth is that this is simply a common symptom of severe anxiety.

We can also program our brains about *what* to respond to. Consider the example of first-time parents with their new baby. Before the baby came along they may have been able to sleep through the night without waking despite ticking clocks, barking dogs, passing cars and maybe even planes and trains. We hear these things because our ears never stop working, but our brain considers it background noise of no importance, and so we do not wake. Yet once the baby comes along, the parents, and usually particularly the mother, will wake in response to any noise from the baby. Not just crying, but snuffling, coughing and other soft sounds—much quieter sounds than she formerly slept through without being disturbed.

The difference is explained by the mother's unconscious programming. Since ticking clocks and barking dogs have no particular significance, there is no need for her to wake (or to be alerted by the brain so that she does wake). But most first-time parents are understandably anxious about their tiny baby. Unconsciously, they program their brain: 'I want to know about it if *anything* happens with this baby.' Accordingly, at the slightest sound, the brain alerts them and they wake up.

Paying particular attention to certain stimuli and not others in the environment can contribute to excessive worry and anxiety if the concerns are unreasonable. Hypervigilant individuals pay too much attention to external factors or internal sensations that they find threatening in some way.

For example, Jenny pays too much attention to her headaches and anxiety, which only reinforces her beliefs that she has a serious medical condition (a brain tumour). If you have programmed your brain to interpret certain events or situations as threatening, and this programming does not reflect the reality of the situation, you will need to reprogram your brain as part of your anxiety management program. This is done through a combination of cognitive challenging and attention refocusing (discussed in chapters eleven and twelve).

Cognitive restructuring

In cognitive challenging it is necessary to first identify how you are interpreting situations that make you anxious or upset. In many cases your interpretations will represent the 'programs' that you have written over the years to guide your brain in its automatic and rapid processing of information. Many writers refer to this as 'automatic thinking'. We tend to have such programs or beliefs about ourselves, the world, our relationships and many situations in which we regularly find ourselves. When you later examine these beliefs or programs in detail, you may find that some are faulty and need to be rewritten. We call this step of cognitive challenging 'cognitive restructuring'. By repeatedly reviewing your beliefs and interpretations of events and rewriting them, your programs will eventually be 'restructured' and the new beliefs will become habitual. You will have created new, more realistic and more helpful ways of thinking about and responding to situations that formerly made you very anxious, such as when you need to make a decision or when you are facing considerable uncertainty.

An analogy might be going to see a golf professional or tennis coach to improve your game. Let's say you wanted to improve your golf swing and decided to get some lessons from your local course professional. The first thing the professional would probably do is ask you to hit a few balls while he watches your swing. Because he's skilled at coaching he would be able to identify the parts of your swing that don't work well for you. The next thing he would probably do is suggest some alternative movements for those that don't work well. He would then ask you to practise these small segments of your swing over and over again, to try to make them come smoothly to you. Then you would be asked to put it all together and try out your full swing, incorporating the new movements. At first your swing would probably be quite awkward, and possibly less effective than it was before. With continued practice, however, it would all come together and eventually you would be able to do the new movements automatically, without having to think about them. Your swing would be greatly improved and you'd enjoy your game more. You would have invested time and effort in practising, and spent money on the lessons. The pay off would be that you achieved your goal of having a better swing and would be able to enjoy your game more.

In cognitive restructuring you follow the same rather tedious steps of analysing your programs, taking out the unhelpful parts and substituting more helpful strategies. Then you put it all together and practise, practise, practise.

IDENTIFYING THOUGHTS

One point that needs to be stressed is that our interpretations of the situations we find ourselves in are made almost instantly. The way we think about a situation will in turn be the prime determinant of how we feel emotionally. Because our thinking about (interpreting, processing) a situation happens instantly we are usually not aware of this step. Instead, the first thing we tend to notice is that we feel anxious or upset about something. In order to uncover your own unhelpful programming or beliefs about situations, yourself and the world, you will need to sit down later and review your reactions. You will need to play detective and try to recapture the thoughts that flashed through your mind in response to challenging experiences or situations. Although this thinking happened rapidly and outside your awareness at the time, it is usually possible to access those thoughts later with careful scrutiny.

It may help to remember that your thoughts will always match your feelings. So even though the emotional reaction may appear unusual or out of proportion to the situation, once the thoughts that occurred in response to the situation are known, the reaction will make sense. Consider the example that was given on page 50, where we saw three different reactions to winning a trip away. On the surface of it, it seems odd that anyone should be upset by this event. But once we understand that for one person it was a painful reminder of a lost relationship, their reaction immediately makes sense.

Some emotions link frequently to particular themes. For example, people who feel sad are frequently experiencing, or remembering, a loss of some type. This could be the loss of a relationship, of health, a job, or even a sense of lost opportunity. Angry feelings are frequently linked to thoughts of having been treated badly in some way. Usually, there is a sense that this was through someone else's carelessness or even deliberate action. Examples include feeling unfairly passed over for promotion, believing that someone has not done their share of the work, or believing that someone has spread unpleasant and untrue gossip about us. Anxious feelings are usually associated with thoughts of being under some kind of threat, as we have discussed previously in this book. We can perceive many types of threat, including threats to our health and physical safety, to our jobs and relationships, to our peace of mind and to our reputation.

Some experiences and situations may be associated with feelings of several kinds. For example, when someone arranges to meet us then fails to turn up, we may feel both angry and disappointed. Before going away to camp many children feel both anxious and excited. Hearing from someone who used to be a close friend but whom you had not heard from for many years may lead you to feel a mixture of curiosity, excitement, apprehension, anger and sadness! It all depends on what you're thinking. Let's look more closely at this example.

Imagine that you run into an old flame at a party. You went out with this person for a couple of years and would have liked to marry them, but they seemed to get cold feet. You drifted apart five years ago and haven't heard from them since. Imagine the mixture of feelings you might experience when you run into them—surprise, curiosity, awkwardness, sadness, anger and regret could be some reactions. You would probably be aware of these feelings before you would any thoughts. Yet there would be thoughts behind the feelings. These might include:

Thoughts	Feelings
Oh my goodness! Can that really be …?	Surprise
I wonder what he's doing now.	Curiosity
I wonder if she's with anyone else.	
I wonder what he feels about me now.	
I don't know what to say to her!	Awkwardness
I was so sad when we broke up.	Sadness
I spent an important part of my life with him.	
It was such a pity it didn't work out.	Regret
It was pathetic that she couldn't commit.	Anger
How could she treat me that way after I invested so much of myself in that relationship!	

Once you have identified the underlying thoughts you can go on to challenge them. The easiest way to implement this process is to notice any feelings of emotional discomfort or distress and then work through the following steps:

1. Notice feelings of distress or emotional discomfort.
2. Describe these feelings as accurately as possible.
3. Rate the strength of these feelings (refer to the Subjective Units of Distress given below).
4. Think back to what might have triggered these feelings. You can ask yourself:
   a. What was I just doing?
   b. Did I just hear something upsetting?
   c. Did I have an uncomfortable feeling or thought?
5. Now try to identify the thoughts behind the feelings.
6. Challenge your thoughts:
   a. Are they realistic?
   b. Are they helpful?

It is useful for several reasons to rate the strength of the emotions you are experiencing. The 'strength' of the thought will be closely related to the strength of the emotion. For example, feeling nervous compared to feeling terrified; feeling irritated compared to feeling enraged. Feeling nervous relates to thoughts that perhaps something unpleasant but not too serious could possibly happen. Feeling terrified is more likely to be associated with a thought like 'I'm going to die.' The Subjective Units of Distress (or SUDs) scale is usually used for this purpose. You can give your feelings a score between 0 and 100. Some anchor points are shown below for guidance, but you can choose any number. Do try to be consistent in your ratings. For example, you can't be suffering the 'worst ever' anxiety every time! Try to neither overestimate nor underestimate.

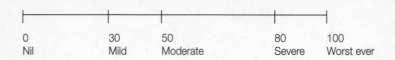

| | 0 | 30 | 50 | 80 | 100 |
| Nil | Mild | Moderate | Severe | Worst ever |

Figure 10.1: Subjective Units of Distress (SUDs)

If we go back to the example given above we might now add the following SUDs:

Thoughts	Feelings	SUDs
Oh my goodness! Can that really be … ?	Surprise	60
I wonder what he's doing now. I wonder if she's with anyone else. I wonder what he feels about me now.	Curiosity	30
I don't know what to say to her!	Awkwardness	70
I was so sad when we broke up. I spent an important part of my life with him.	Sadness	50
It was a pity it didn't work out.	Regret	45

It was pathetic that she couldn't commit.
How could she treat me that way after I
  invested so much of myself in that
  relationship!
	Anger	55

None of these SUDS are too severe, so it would be safe to assume that you were probably over the worst of your disappointment and had moved on. Look at the thought that goes with the feelings of regret: 'It was a pity it didn't work out.' Had the level of regret been 80, for example, then we might have expected a thought more like, 'It was a terrible disappointment that it didn't work out.' Or with even higher SUDs of 90 to 100, there might be thoughts like,

'I was devastated when this relationship failed. I still feel affected by it.' In this way the thoughts match the feelings.

THE ABC OF REALISTIC THINKING

It always helps to have a structure, and cognitive challenging has an easy-to-remember formula of A-B-C-D-E. The letters are intended to remind you of the following components of cognitive challenging:

A: The *activating* event or trigger.
This can be a situation, a thought or a feeling.

B: Your *beliefs* (or the interpretations you make) about the activating event.

C: The emotional *consequences* of these beliefs for you.

D: You then *dispute* or challenge these beliefs, and generate more helpful and realistic beliefs about the activating event or situation.

E: You may design *experiments* to test your beliefs. Otherwise this column may be used to record an outcome or simply to re-*evaluate* the strength of your emotions after disputing or challenging your beliefs.

In the example we have been discussing, the activating event would be running into your old flame at a party. Thus our table would look as follows.

A: Activating event or situation	B: Beliefs, thoughts or interpretation	C: Consequences, feelings	
Running into [name] at Jill's party.	Oh my goodness! Can that really be … ?	Surprise	60
	I wonder what he's doing now.	Curiosity	30
	I wonder if she's with anyone else.		
	I wonder what he feels about me now.		
	I don't know what to say to her!	Awkwardness	70
	I was so sad when we broke up.	Sadness	60
	I spent an important part of my life with him.		
	It was such a pity that it didn't work out.	Regret	45
	It was pathetic that she couldn't commit.	Anger	55
	How could she treat me that way after I invested so much of myself in that relationship?		

Before we go on to cognitive challenging, it would be helpful for you to try one or two of these exercises for yourself. Start by drawing up three columns on a worksheet or in the exercise book you obtained previously for your worry diary. Label the columns the same as in the example above so that you can remind yourself what the A-B-C headings stand for. Next, think back to a time recently when you felt anxious or upset in some way. It might be best to start with something that was only mildly upsetting. In column C record all the feelings you can identify. Try to get the exact nuance of the emotion—for example, did you feel nervous, scared, terrified, panicky? Did you feel a sense of dread? Rate the strength of *each* emotion separately, referring to the SUDs scale.

Now try to think what might have triggered these feelings. If you were feeling worried and anxious, refer back to your worry diary. Was it one of the triggers that you identified there? If you're having trouble identifying the activating event or trigger, try to think back to what was happening around that time. Common triggers that people report include:

- conversations with people
- hearing something on the news
- reading something in a magazine
- having a particular task to perform.

If the experience in question was too long ago to remember clearly, it might be better to start with something more recent, or even to see what happens over the next few days. It is easier to identify your thinking when it is fresh in your mind. I have included some examples below.

Tracey

Tracey, 52, worries whenever her husband is late coming home from work. She becomes convinced that he must have had an accident. This makes her extremely anxious and upset.

Here is one of Tracey's A-B-C exercises.

A: Activating event or situation	B: Beliefs, thoughts or interpretation	C: Consequences, feelings	
My husband was 20 minutes late home and has not called.	Why hasn't he called? There must have been an accident. He must be hurt and that's why he hasn't called. What if he is seriously injured? How will I cope?	Anxiety	80

Note that the thoughts are expressed in sentences rather than shorthand. That is, rather than just 'could be hurt', the full concern is expressed. This will make it easier to do the cognitive challenging later.

Nick

Nick, 27, is an electrician who worries about making mistakes. He checks his work carefully but also worries that, despite checking it, he may somehow still have missed something important. He also worries about unexpected problems or difficulties that could arise, and dreads having to make a decision about something himself, in case he gets it 'wrong'.

He identified the trigger to a worry episode as shown below.

A: Activating event or situation	B: Beliefs, thoughts or interpretation	C: Consequences, feelings	
The boss asked to talk to me about a job I did.	What if I have made a mistake?	Anxiety	80
		Dread	90
		Disappointment	80

Have a good look at this example. Does it make immediate sense to you why a thought of 'What if I have made a mistake?' should cause such severe levels of anxiety? Why should it lead to a feeling of disappointment? When you read Nick's A-B-C you may have thought, 'I don't get this one.' That's because this example is incomplete. Not all the thoughts have been identified. You can tell this because the thought doesn't fit the feelings like a hand in a glove. You don't get that feeling of complete understanding the way you did (hopefully) with the other examples. Often, we are only aware of the most superficial thoughts in our head, but these may not be the main cause of our anxiety.

One way to try to track down the root of the worry is to ask, 'Why would that matter?' or 'What would happen then?' If we ask these questions in Nick's case we might find the following trail:

A: Activating event or situation	B: Beliefs, thoughts or interpretation	C: Consequences, feelings	
The boss asked to talk to me about a job I did.	What if I have made a mistake?	Anxiety	80
	▼	Dread	90
	The boss will be angry.	Disappointment	80
	▼		
	He will not want to keep me on.		
	▼		
	I won't get a good reference from him.		
	▼		
	I won't get another job as an electrician again.		
	▼		
	I won't be able to do what I really enjoy in life and will be miserable.		
	▼		
	I won't be able to buy my own house or be independent. I promised myself I would be extra careful with this job— I've let myself down again.		

Does this seem to match the feelings better now? This technique of looking for the underlying fear is sometimes called the 'downward arrow' technique, or the 'chain of thoughts', to indicate how one thought leads to another. It's amazing to think that this happens in a fraction of a second inside your head!

Similarly, 'what if …' isn't the end of the story, either. There are usually unrealised fears that underlie the 'what if …' and that are the real source of concern. On page 39 you read about Stan who could not decide whether or not to take a redundancy package. Stan's chain of thoughts was, 'What if we suddenly needed a lot of money for something? What if I can't get another job? What if my wife gets sick and can't work? What if we get into financial difficulties as a result of my leaving work—it would be all my fault. I would have failed in my role as a husband and provider and we would end up destitute.'

It turned out that all his life Stan had worried about being a good provider. His father had brought him up to see this as his primary responsibility and 'the measure of a man'. However, Stan wasn't aware that this was his real fear until we explored it in therapy. Up until then, he just thought he was worried about making the decision. The rest of his fear was subconscious—but open to discovery with a little detective work. With a fear this big, it's no wonder his worry was severe.

It is important to be as thorough as you can in identifying all the thoughts you have in relation to a trigger. If you don't identify a thought, you can't challenge it. This means it can go on causing anxiety and distress.

It does take practice to master the skill of identifying your thoughts. Try a couple of examples based on your own experiences. If you have difficulty in identifying your cognitions, imagine yourself trying to explain them to someone who didn't know anything about you or why you felt upset or worried. If it is still difficult for you, it might help to see a therapist with CBT training. Once you have a couple of examples to work with, you can try using the cognitive challenging techniques described in the next chapter.

Chapter Eleven

COGNITIVE CHALLENGING

Cognitive challenging is a technique to help you think as helpfully and realistically as possible. This makes life easier! Again, you need to be thorough in order for the technique to be effective in reducing anxiety. The way to achieve this is to take each thought in turn that you identified in your B columns in chapter ten and ask yourself some questions to help you decide whether they are realistic and helpful statements based on facts. If not, then you need to rephrase or even completely change your response. The aim is to develop a realistic and helpful interpretation of the event or situation that triggered worrying thoughts and your subsequent anxiety. This chapter will introduce you to a number of techniques that may be employed to effectively challenge cognitions. So although it may look as though a number of different techniques are being described, remember that they're all ways of achieving the same outcome. Try them all; then adopt the methods that work best for you.

USE THE FACTS, AND ONLY THE FACTS

Often we don't have all the information about a situation. We tend to respond by making assumptions. For example, Sydney trains used to have seats with a back that could be moved to face either direction. Most people prefer to sit with the seat facing in the direction of travel. I boarded the train at an early stop. It was nearly empty and all the seats were facing backwards—obviously this train had an engine at either end and, having reached its furthest destination, was on its way back to the city using the engine that was now at the leading end of the train. I couldn't be bothered turning the back over so that the seat faced forward, and simply sat down. As the train progressively filled, embarking passengers would find an empty seat, turn it to face forward and sit down. No one sat next to me in my backwards facing seat until, eventually, the seat next to me and one opposite it were the only two seats left. Two women came on board and took these seats facing each other. The one sitting next to me immediately said to her companion, 'This seat doesn't move.' Not 'probably' or 'maybe'—she just assumed as fact that the seat didn't move, or else surely I would have moved it! This was a harmless assumption to make—the woman didn't get upset or anxious and the psychiatrist in me found it an interesting illustration of human nature. But some of the assumptions you are making in your life could be causing you unnecessary anxiety or distress. For example, assuming that a headache must be due to a brain tumour, or that you will lose your job if you make a mistake. I suggest that you make it a rule for yourself from now on that you will stick to the facts, and only make interpretations supported by fact. If you don't have facts, then try to get them. If they are not available, then learn to accept what you know and what you don't know, and to manage the anxiety of uncertainty. In other words, a headache is just a headache unless it is proven to be a brain tumour.

Sometimes facts may be hard to accept, because alternative (but incorrect) beliefs may appear much more compelling. The earth really does look flat, doesn't it? You can imagine how hard it was for people to reject the apparent proof right before their eyes and accept something that they couldn't see. It is much easier for us because we have been brought up believing that the earth is round, and there is now ample proof of it, including pictures from space. Keep this lesson in mind.

Sometimes the answer that seems most likely is not the real explanation for something. When you are feeling really anxious it might seem that disaster is just around the corner, but this may not be the case.

ARGUE LIKE A LAWYER

Ask yourself what evidence you have to back up your thoughts. Is there evidence to the contrary? How strong is your evidence? What other interpretations are possible for the observed facts? Remember to stick to the facts! Your arguments need to be strong enough to convince a jury or you should reject them. In the last chapter there was an example from Tracey's workbook. Her husband was 20 minutes late home from work and hadn't called her. She felt worried and realised she was thinking: 'He must have had an accident.' Tracey needs to challenge this belief. Does she have any evidence that her husband has had an accident? No. She has made an assumption. Are there other possible explanations for why her husband might be late? Yes. Write some down for yourself as an exercise in logical thinking before reading on.

Possible explanations for Tracey's husband being late home:

_____

_____

_____

_____

Your alternatives might have included:

- He was a bit late leaving work, but didn't feel it was late enough that Tracey would worry and therefore didn't call.

- He was stuck in traffic.
- He stopped at a shop on the way home.
- He was stuck in a meeting and unable to call.

In another example, Sam worried about giving a presentation at work. He had been working on a project that required considerable research. He was due to present his findings and recommendations at a meeting that was to be attended by his boss and other colleagues from his department. He became extremely worried about the presentation, especially about his boss's reaction. His A-B-C exercise is shown below.

A: Activating event or situation	B: Beliefs, thoughts or interpretation	C: Consequences, feelings	
I have to present my report to my boss and other colleagues.	What if I have missed something important?	Anxiety	80
	▼		
	My boss will think I'm incompetent.		
	▼		
	He probably knows all this information already.		
	▼		
	He will think I'm useless.		
	▼		
	He will not want to renew my contract.		
	▼		
	I won't be able to find another job in this economic climate.		
	▼		
	We'll have to live off our savings.		
	▼		
	We'll never be able to afford to buy a house.		

Let's look at Sam's belief that his boss probably already knows everything Sam is going to present. Sam was asked to present evidence for and against this belief. He came up with the following:

- Evidence for: 'None—just a fear I have.'
- Evidence against: 'My boss has told me that he doesn't know much about this area.'

I think the evidence against would convince a jury! It's the best kind of evidence there is—it's based on fact. His boss has actually told him directly. Sam has no evidence for his original belief; it was an assumption he made based on his fears.

DON'T CONFUSE A POSSIBILITY WITH A PROBABILITY

Worriers often confuse a possibility with a probability, and this is a potent cause of unnecessary worry. How often has the worst possibility actually happened? For most people, the answer is 'rarely'. This means that they spend many, many hours of their life worrying about things that don't happen.

If this is a trap you tend to fall into, it may help you to remember the old saying, 'When you hear hoof beats, think of horses not zebras.' This saying is appropriate for most of the world. However, if you live in some parts of Africa the reverse may be true! And there are probably some parts of the world where you need to think of camels or moose when you hear hoof beats, but you get the picture. It reminds you to be realistic when considering possibilities.

Another recommendation I give my patients is to play the odds. This is just another way of determining what's the most likely explanation. Act as if the most likely explanation is valid and you will save yourself many hours of worry, since the most likely explanation is usually true. The favourite in a horse race *is* more likely to win, and this is why you won't win much money on it! In the same way, a headache is more likely to be the result of tension than it is to be due to a brain tumour. And, more likely than not, you *have* locked the front door.

Importantly, this is how non-worriers deal with uncertainty. They play the odds and assume that the most likely explanation is true. Then, they wait and see. In this way, they'll be right most of the time—that is, the most likely outcome will usually result. In the less common cases where a less likely alternative results, they deal with it when it happens. Remember the old saying, 'Cross that bridge when you come to it'? It's another useful saying when managing worry and anxiety.

Tips to remember

1. Stick to the facts.
2. Argue like a lawyer.
3. Don't confuse a possibility with a probability.
4. When you hear hoof beats, think of horses not zebras.
5. Play the odds.
6. Wait and see.

Keeping these guidelines in mind, let's have a further look at some of the examples we studied in the last chapter, and add column D: cognitive challenging, and column E: experiment. We will employ the principles we've been discussing.

Our first example is from Tracey's workbook (right).

First of all, notice that *each* belief has been challenged. Tracey has employed a number of strategies to challenge her beliefs. These are examined below.

A: Activating event or situation	B: Beliefs, thoughts or interpretation	C: Consequences, feelings		D: Dispute or challenge	E: Experiment or outcome	
My husband was 20 minutes late home and had not called.	Why hasn't he called? ▸ There must have been an accident. ▸ He must be hurt and that's why he hasn't called. What if he is seriously injured? How will I cope? I'm so anxious, there must be something wrong.	Anxiety Dread	80 90	This has happened a number of times before and it's usually because he's stuck in a meeting and can't call. Occasionally, he has stopped in at the local shop and lost track of time. Both of these are much more likely than an accident. Since it's unlikely that he's had an accident, this is probably not the reason why he hasn't called. Even if he has had an accident, it's not likely to be serious—most accidents in the city are relatively minor. When bad things have happened before, I have coped—so I probably would again. I'm anxious because I've been worrying—it's not evidence that there's anything wrong. I've felt anxious lots of times before and nothing bad has actually happened.	Anxiety Dread	30 0

(P) Belief: There must have been an accident.

(R) Technique: *Argue like a lawyer; play the odds*. The evidence is that every time her husband has been late before he's either been stuck in a meeting or stopped off at the shops.

(P) Belief: He must be hurt.

(R) Technique: *Don't confuse a probability and a possibility; play the odds* It's unlikely that he's had an accident, and even if he had, most accidents in the city—where he is driving—are minor.

(P) Belief: How will I cope?

(R) Technique: *Play the odds; wait and see*. Previous experience suggests that she would cope if something bad happened—even though this is not the most likely explanation for her husband being late. Therefore, on the balance of probabilities, she would probably cope this time if she had to.

(P) Belief: Feeling anxious is evidence something is wrong.

(R) Technique: *Argue like a lawyer*. We feel anxious in response to worrying thoughts as part of the flight or fight response—it's not because we're psychic.

In this case we don't really have any facts—only the facts that her husband is late and hasn't called. There is therefore uncertainty, and this is anxiety provoking. By using cognitive challenging techniques Tracey controls her anxious imagination and restricts herself to probabilities and realistic thinking. When she reviews the challenges she has generated (in column D), Tracey can now re-rate the emotions she experienced in response to her beliefs (column B). Tracey copies 'anxiety' and 'dread' to column E and re-rates them while keeping in mind her challenges from column D. Her new ratings are 30 for anxiety and 0 for dread. In other words, she realises that there is no basis in reality to feel any dread, although she is still mildly anxious about her husband being late home.

There is another technique that Tracey could have used to help her choose the most likely explanation. She could have estimated the actual probability of each potential explanation. Firstly, she could try to estimate the probability of an accident. Her thought processes might look something like this:

(P) For how many years has Steve been driving?
(R) 20 years

(P) On average, how many trips does he make per week (out and back counts as two trips)?
(R) 16 trips

(P) How many trips does he make per year, on average?
(R) 800 trips

(P) How many accidents has he had?
(R) Two accidents

(P) How many of these have been serious?
(R) None

From this we can make a rough estimate that Steve has made 16 000 trips in his driving career and has had two accidents, neither of them serious. His risk of an accident is therefore 2/16 000—or 0.0125 per cent—and his risk of a serious accident is close to zero. (We can't say it *is* zero, even though he hasn't had any serious accidents, because it is possible—although very unlikely.)

Now let's examine the probability of the first alternative that Tracey generated—that Steve may be stuck in a meeting.

(P) On average, how many times per month is Steve late home?
(R) Three times

(P) What is the yearly average of being late home?
(R) 36 times

(P) On average, how often each month is Steve late home because of a meeting?
(R) Two to three times

(P) What is the yearly average of being late home because of a meeting?

(R) 24 to 36 times (average is 30)

Hence we can conclude that approximately 30 out of 36 times that Steve is late, it is because he is stuck in a meeting. The likelihood that this is the true explanation for him being late is thus 83 per cent. This is a *much* more likely explanation than an accident.

OTHER STRATEGIES FOR COGNITIVE CHALLENGING

Another way to apply the cognitive challenging techniques discussed above, is to ask yourself a number of questions about each of your beliefs:

- What is the evidence for and against?
- What alternative explanations are there?
- How likely is the feared outcome really?

Let's see how these questions can be used in an example taken from Nick, the electrician. Nick's first effort in his workbook is shown on the opposite page.

In this case Nick can ask himself the challenging questions. For practice, he should ask each challenging question about each thought, in order to develop the habit of being thorough. If the question doesn't really seem to apply, he can go on to the next one.

(P) Belief: What if I have made a mistake?

(R) Challenging questions:

What is the evidence for and against? There is no evidence either way—the boss could have asked to see me for any number of reasons.

What alternative explanations are there? The boss may want to see me for a number of reasons: to simply discuss the job or even give me another. There

A: Activating event or situation	B: Beliefs, thoughts or interpretation	C: Consequences, feelings	
The boss asked to talk to me about a job I did.	What if I have made a mistake?	Anxiety	80
	▼	Dread	90
	The boss will be angry.	Disappointment	80
	▼		
	He will not want to keep me on.		
	▼		
	I won't get a good reference from him.		
	▼		
	I won't get another job as an electrician again.		
	▼		
	I won't be able to do what I really enjoy in life and will be miserable.		
	▼		
	I won't be able to buy my own house or be independent. I promised myself I would be extra careful with this job— I've let myself down again.		

was some trouble with the client when the booking was made, so maybe he wants to know whether it went smoothly.

How likely is it that I have made a mistake? I occasionally make minor mistakes, but 95 per cent of the time I pick them up when I check my work. I have never made a serious mistake.

(P) Belief: The boss will be angry.

(R) Challenging questions:

What is the evidence for and against? The boss does get angry sometimes, so it is possible—but it is usually when he feels that people have been lazy or careless. He has told me that he values my work.

What alternative explanations are there? If I made a mistake the boss could be quite understanding—I have seen this happen with others.

How likely is it that the boss will be angry? Since I'm unlikely to have made a serious mistake, and I'm certainly not careless or lazy, it's probably unlikely.

(P) Belief: He will not want to keep me on.
(R) Challenging questions:

What is the evidence for and against? There is no evidence for this.

What alternative explanations are there? That he will want to keep me on. That if I have made a mistake he will just want to talk about it and help me realise it so I don't make it again.

How likely is it that the boss will not want to keep me on? Even if I have made a mistake it is very unlikely that I would get the sack.

Nick would go on to challenge each of his thoughts in this way. This may seem like a lot of work, but it does help the process to become effective and automatic. It can be helpful to generate a summary in the end such as: 'It is very unlikely that I have made a mistake, and even if I have, it is unlikely to be serious and it is unlikely that the boss will be angry or want to sack me.'

Nick can now create an A-B-C-D-E exercise in his workbook as shown right.

Note that Nick's worry, anxiety and disappointment do not go down to zero. Tracey's anxiety went down to 30 but did not disappear completely. Some worry and anxiety is a normal part of life. The aim of cognitive challenging is to make sure that you do not suffer excessive amounts of anxiety that are out of proportion to the situation.

If Nick's worries recur later, he can simply repeat his summary and then stop himself from engaging in any further worry.

Look at Nick's last belief, 'I promised myself I would be extra careful with this job—I've let myself down again.' This should be challenged in the same way as the others, but there are some extra questions that can be helpful with this sort of self-critical belief.

A: Activating event or situation	B: Beliefs, thoughts or interpretation	C: Consequences, feelings	D: Dispute or challenge	E: Experiment or outcome
The boss asked to talk to me about a job I did.	What if I have made a mistake? ▸ The boss will be angry. ▸ He will not want to keep me on. ▸ I won't get a good reference from him. ▸ I won't get another job as an electrician again. ▸ I won't be able to do what I really enjoy in life and will be miserable. ▸ I won't be able to buy my own house or be independent. I promised myself I would be extra careful with this job— I've let myself down again.	Anxiety 80 Dread 90 Disappointment 80	I occasionally make minor mistakes, but 95 per cent of the time I pick them up when I check my work. I have never made a serious mistake. The boss may want to see me for a number of reasons: to simply discuss the job or even give me another. There was some trouble with the client when the booking was made, so maybe he wants to know whether it went smoothly. The boss does get angry sometimes, so it is possible—but it is usually when he feels that people have been lazy or careless. He has told me that he values my work. He would not withhold a reference from me for an honest mistake, and he wouldn't sack me for this either. Even if I didn't get a reference I could work for myself. It is very unlikely that I have made a mistake, and even if I have, it is unlikely to be serious and it is unlikely that the boss will be angry or want to sack me.	Anxiety 40 Dread 20 Disappointment 40

- How much do I have to let it matter?
- How do I gain by thinking this way?
- How do I lose by thinking this way?
- What would I say to someone else who was in this position?

The first question is a reminder that we can choose how to react to something that happens. Our reaction is determined by how we think about what happens to us, and we can exert control over how we choose to think. The next two questions are designed to help us remain aware of how our thinking can affect our emotional state.

(P) Belief: I promised myself I would be extra careful with this job—I've let myself down again.

(R) Challenging questions:

What is the evidence for and against? I was very careful with this job. Even if I have made a mistake it doesn't mean I've let myself down, since my goal was to be careful and I was.

What alternative explanations are there? [This question doesn't apply easily here.]

How likely is it that I've let myself down? [Already answered above.]

How much do I have to let it matter? It's not the end of the world even if I hadn't been as careful as I would have liked—there will be other opportunities. Even making a mistake is not the end of the world—often it's just minor and does no real harm. No one is perfect.

How do I gain by thinking this way? It feels as though it will make me more motivated to do well—but I am always careful anyway.

How do I lose by thinking this way? It really puts me under pressure and makes me anxious.

What would I say to someone else? I would tell them that no one can do more than their best.

There is one further question that may be used with care by excessive worriers, and this is:

- What's the worst thing that could happen?

Sometimes we become extremely anxious about an event or situation *without* identifying what we're actually afraid of. When you hear yourself saying things like, 'I won't cope' or 'What if it goes wrong?' it can be helpful to ask yourself exactly what you're afraid of. These undefined worries can hang over our heads like big black clouds. We can respond to them as if they are catastrophes waiting to happen. But sometimes, when you look more closely at your thoughts, and try to pin down exactly what you're frightened of, you may find that the worst thing that can happen is really not so bad. You may also see that it is an unrealistic fear.

Even when your worst fear is pretty bad, it's still easier to deal with something concrete than a big nameless fear. You can't take any steps to prevent or prepare for something that you haven't even identified. Remember that there really isn't anything you can't face the thought of, even though you might think there is. Has there in reality ever been a thought that sent you crazy? When you face the worst, there is pretty much nothing else that can scare you. And you can begin to take real control, rather than continue the illusion of being in control through worry.

Recognising the unhelpfulness of certain patterns of thinking can assist you to avoid using them in the future. It is common for people to develop a habit of thinking in a certain way because it feels as though it might be helpful. In reality, it may be quite unhelpful. Nick's tendency to expect himself to do a job perfectly is a good example. It seemed to him that thinking in this way would be motivating, but, since no one can be perfect, it often results in him feeling disappointed in himself and worried about his performance. This is another illustration of the value of challenging your beliefs as comprehensively as you can. It also illustrates the need for careful scrutiny of your underlying beliefs if you are suffering from excessive levels of emotional distress, whether depression, anxiety or anger. You may be unaware of the unhelpful beliefs and patterns of thinking that are making life more difficult for you.

COGNITIVE 'ERRORS'

Cognitive 'errors' are common patterns of unhelpful thinking. By learning to recognise these patterns it may help you to avoid them. Some people also find this a helpful approach to cognitive challenging.

(P) Cognitive error: Catastrophising
(R) Characterised by: You blow things out of proportion or assume the worst.

(P) Cognitive error: Awfulising
(R) Characterised by: 'That would be awful! I couldn't stand it!' You blow out of proportion how much something would affect you.

(P) Cognitive error: Black and white thinking
(R) Characterised by: You see things as either good or bad, right or wrong. You are not able to appreciate compromises and grey areas.

(P) Cognitive error: Focusing on the negative
(R) Characterised by: You ignore the positive signs and only take notice of negatives.

(P) Cognitive error: Personalising
(R) Characterised by: You see everything as being your fault or directed at you.

(P) Cognitive error: Fortune telling
(R) Characterised by: You predict the future (usually negatively). For example, 'I won't cope', 'I'll fail'.

(P) Cognitive error: Perfectionism
(R) Characterised by: 'If it isn't perfect, it's no good at all.' If it isn't perfect, you believe you're worthless, unlovable or a failure.

(P) Cognitive error: Jumping to conclusions
(R) Characterised by: You make assumptions, without any corroborating evidence. For example, 'The palpitations mean there's something wrong with my heart.' 'The boss wants to see me; I must have made a mistake.'

(P) Cognitive error: Emotional reasoning
(R) Characterised by: You use an emotion as evidence of a belief. For example, believing that something must be wrong simply because you feel anxious.

(The real explanation is that you are anxious because you are worrying—it is fear that has caused your anxiety.) This is a very common cognitive error in cases of excessive worry.

In the patient case examples looked at in this chapter we can see evidence of *catastrophising* in both Tracey's belief that her husband must be seriously injured in a car accident and Nick's belief that he will lose his job over a mistake that he probably hasn't even made. They both indulge in *fortune telling* with Tracey saying, 'I won't cope', and Nick thinking, 'The boss will be angry.' They both *jump to conclusions*—Tracey believes that her husband's failure to call means he's injured, and Nick is convinced that he must have done something wrong. Nick is also demonstrating *perfectionism* in his expectations of himself in the job. Tracey is using *emotional reasoning* by seeing her anxiety as evidence that something must be wrong.

A *practice example*

Let's look at an A-B-C example from Jenny's workbook. Jenny worries unreasonably that her headaches might be a brain tumour.

A: Activating event or situation	B: Beliefs, thoughts or interpretation	C: Consequences, feelings	
I notice I have a headache.	Maybe this time it really is a brain tumour.	Anxiety	70
		Sadness	80
	▼		
	I will die.		
	▼		
	My children will be left without a mother.		
	▼		
	They will never recover from such a loss.		

Now see if you can add a D column to Jenny's example by applying the guidelines of sticking to the facts, arguing like a lawyer and playing the odds. You can do this by asking challenging questions and looking for cognitive errors. Try to generate some cognitive challenges for these beliefs before reading on.

Jenny wrote down her cognitive challenging in her workbook. This is shown below:

(P) Belief: What if my headache is a brain tumour?

(R) Challenging questions:

What is the evidence for and against? Although theoretically a headache could be caused by a brain tumour, I have no evidence that I have a brain tumour. On the contrary, I have good evidence from all the tests and from seeing all the doctors and specialists that I do not have a brain tumour.

What would I tell someone else in this position? I would tell them that this proved they did not have a brain tumour.

What alternative explanations are there? There are several other possible explanations for my headaches. Sometimes they could be migraines or tension headaches. I might also get a headache because of worrying so much.

How likely is a brain tumour? Brain tumours are very rare, especially in my age group. Given the fact that some very powerful tests have failed to find a brain tumour, it makes it virtually impossible for me to have a tumour.

How much do I have to let it matter? Obviously, it would be a bad thing to have a brain tumour, but I guess the point is that I don't need to keep thinking about it.

How do I gain by thinking this way? I feel compelled to think about it, as if it might save my life. I wouldn't want to totally ignore physical symptoms, but there must be some point in the middle that balances a healthy awareness with excessive worrying.

How do I lose by thinking this way? I am constantly anxious because I constantly worry about it. I now have trouble telling the difference between something that I really should be worried about, and something that is just a normal symptom that people get, like headaches.

What's the worst thing that could happen? I don't even like to think about this. The worst that could happen is that I could be in terrible pain and die, and leave my children without a mother. However, if I do think about it rationally, many types of brain tumour can be successfully treated these days. If it was a tumour, it could be benign rather than malignant anyway. And although it would definitely not be the best thing for my children to lose me, at least they would still have their father who loves them very much.

Jenny could summarise all this by saying: 'It is most likely that my headache is the result of tension or anxiety, since all the tests I've had and all the specialists I've seen have failed to find any tumour. It would be most helpful to me to stop focusing on my head and get on with my life.'

Jenny's thinking demonstrates evidence of *jumping to conclusions*. She automatically assumes a headache is coming from a brain tumour. Not only is there no evidence for this, there is evidence to the contrary! She ignores this evidence and *focuses on the negative*—her headache and her anxious worries. Jenny *catastrophises* about the likely outcome.

GETTING STARTED ON YOUR OWN COGNITIVE CHALLENGING

Now you can begin to identify and challenge your own beliefs. Set the questions and answers out in any way that is helpful to you, but do write down your thinking, and create a summary at the end. Take note over the next week of any uncomfortable feelings or distressing emotions that you experience. These are a signal that you may have over-reacted to something, or may be thinking in some unhelpful or unrealistic way about a situation or event. Work backwards from the emotions to try to identify what may have triggered the feelings: an event, problem or situation you found yourself in, or perhaps an interaction with someone, or just something that reminded you of your worries. Once you have identified the trigger, see if you can go on to identify the cognitions (beliefs or interpretation of the event) that occurred in response to the trigger. The next step is to use the challenging questions and techniques outlined above to challenge your own thoughts. The aim is to reappraise the situation and draw conclusions that are realistic. If you don't know the answer for sure, you can choose to think about the situation in the most helpful way. For example, if I meet someone new and find myself worrying about whether they enjoyed talking to me, there is probably no way to know for sure. I can choose to assume that things went well.

Troubleshooting

(P) 'I'm anxious about writing my thoughts down.'

(R) Some people are frightened to write down their thoughts. They feel as though saying them right out in the open might bring bad luck. It might somehow make their fears come true. This is an example of 'magical thinking', which was explored on page 78.

(P) 'Why bother? It probably won't work anyway.'

(R) Some people are reluctant to try the cognitive challenging because they are pessimistic about it being helpful. Several cognitive errors are evident with this thinking: pessimism (focusing on the negative) and fortune telling. If you don't try cognitive challenging, it definitely won't work; but if you do try it, it just might be helpful. Remember that in overcoming anxiety every little bit helps, so even if it just works a little, you're still ahead.

(P) 'I don't really believe my challenges.'

(R) Many people do not feel really convinced by their challenges. The good news is that this doesn't matter! The key is to *act as if* you do. In other words, if Tracey's challenges conclude that the most likely explanation for her husband's lateness is a meeting, then she should act as if she believes this. She can do this by not engaging further with the worry that he has had an accident, and she should focus her attention on something else—cook dinner, watch television, play with the children, or go for a walk.

(P) 'My SUDs ratings have not gone down.'

(R) If this happens, it most likely means that you have missed a significant belief underlying your anxiety. Re-read chapter ten on how to identify your cognitions. Often our deepest fears are difficult to identify. Once you start to see some patterns emerging in your own worries, you can make sure you look for these every time. For example, fears of failure, responsibility, illness and death are common. Are any of these typical for you?

(P) 'All this writing down sounds as though it is going to be rather tedious.'

(R) You're right! However, it's not forever. The eventual aim is for you to be able to do this kind of realistic thinking instantly and automatically, while you're actually in the situation. This won't happen unless you get plenty of practice. By writing down your thinking and reasoning in a structured way you will train yourself to do it well. This means that it will be *effective*. There's no right and wrong with cognitive challenging. The only tests are:

- Is it helpful?
- Is it realistic?
- Does it work?

The aim of cognitive challenging is for you to think as helpfully and realistically as possible about situations and events in your life. A wide range of techniques has been developed to assist in the process. Experiment with these techniques and choose the ones that help you to identify and challenge your worries effectively. (The test of effectiveness is that your SUDs will reduce.)

In order to develop your skill at cognitive challenging you will need to practise it often. Although it is time consuming, I highly recommend that you do a series of written exercises, working through the steps above and using the A-B-C-D-E format. Remember the example of changing your tennis serve or your golf swing. It takes considerable practice and attention to detail to achieve a good result, but the benefit is that the new technique will be permanent and will happen smoothly and automatically when you need it. Consider your time and effort now as an investment in a calmer future.

Chapter Twelve

NOW STOP WORRYING ABOUT IT

Several chapters ago when I presented the Worry Control Blueprint you saw that the final step was 'Then stop worrying about it!' You probably thought that if you could do that you wouldn't need this book! Undoubtedly you have been told countless times by well-meaning friends and relatives: 'Don't worry about it!' If you could stop worrying, you would—the trouble is that you don't know how.

Knowing how to stop worrying about something is a skill in itself. Many people are lucky, as it comes naturally to them. But it's important to know that you can *learn* this skill. You can train yourself to respond differently to worrying thoughts, and to let go of worries when they do occur. It just takes practice.

THE PRINCIPLES OF HABIT REVERSAL

Worrying is a habit. As we have seen in previous chapters, it is a pattern that you unconsciously developed to cope with uncertainty in life. Worrying seemed to be a helpful strategy, it became a habit, and so you kept using it. I am now suggesting that, in future, when you are faced with uncertainty and fear, you break the worry habit and instead follow the steps in the Worry Control Blueprint.

Any habit can be broken or changed. Examples of habits that people seek to change include nail biting, hair pulling and using certain expressions (particularly children!). In these cases we often wish to completely stop the habitual behaviour. It is also common to want to change habitual ways of doing things, such as a tennis serve, golf swing or swim stroke. In these examples the desire is usually to substitute one behaviour for another—a poor tennis serve for a more effective one. In worry control the aim is to substitute your current worry habit for more effective and less distressing behaviours.

If all we had to do was decide we wanted to do something in order to be able to do it life would be much easier, but we all know that's not really the way things are. It takes concerted and sustained effort to change behaviour. There are several steps that must be followed if a habit is to be broken or changed. These are:

- Make the decision to stop or change the behaviour.
- Monitor yourself for the unwanted behaviour.
- Catch yourself engaging in the behaviour you wish to stop or change.
- Immediately stop and/or substitute the desired behaviour.
- Be consistent—stop the behaviour immediately and stop every time.

Let's apply these principles to nail biting. The first step is to decide that you want to stop biting your nails. Next, you need to be on the lookout for this behaviour. Ideally, you don't want to let yourself start nail biting at all but, in practice, this isn't possible initially so you monitor yourself. You try to do this monitoring in the background rather than focusing on it—after all, you have many other things that require your attention. Typically, you will start to bite your nails without even realising that you're doing it. This is especially likely to occur when you are distracted or bored (such as while watching television, waiting at traffic lights or reading). In fact, you could become more effective at catching yourself in the act of nail biting—and therefore control the habit sooner—by recognising typical trigger situations. You would then be able to be especially vigilant in these situations, or even ensure that your hands were otherwise occupied, since nail biting is much less likely to occur if you are using your hands for something else. For example, when sitting in traffic you could keep both hands on the wheel at all times. When watching television you could hold something in your hands, hold your hands together or even sit on them.

Now let's imagine that at some point you become aware you're biting your nails. It's essential that you stop immediately. It won't improve matters if you say to yourself, 'I'll just finish off this bit of nail.' If you consistently stop yourself as soon as you become aware of biting your nails, you will start to find that you catch yourself earlier and earlier. In time, you will be able to catch yourself *before* you start to bite your nails. Eventually, you will have broken the habit and may not even get the urge to bite your nails any more (although if you did, it would be a lot easier to resist than it used to be).

Changing a physical behaviour is definitely easier than changing a mental behaviour, like worrying. However, it can be done, and very effectively! Let's look at the steps.

Presumably you've made the decision to stop worrying if you're still reading this far. That's the first step taken care of. You've already had some practice at catching yourself worrying, if you completed the worry diary in chapter six. That's the second and third steps dealt with. You will also have a good idea of typical worry triggers, so you can be alert for your reactions in these situations, or even plan to deal with them differently. In order to control your worry you are aiming to substitute the series of behaviours in the Worry Control Blueprint for the old habit of worrying. That is, whenever you find yourself worrying, you go through the steps in the Worry Control Blueprint:

- Ask yourself: 'Is the worry or fear realistic?' Apply your cognitive challenging skills if you're not sure.
- If your worry is realistic, ask yourself: 'Can something be done about it?' Apply your structured problem solving skills if you're not sure. If something can be done about it, do it!
- If your worry is not realistic, if there's nothing you can do about it or if you've done whatever you can, then stop worrying about it!

How do we stop worrying about something? It's important at this point to remember our discussion about thoughts on page 94. You can't stop thoughts from popping into your head, and some of these thoughts will be worries. What you *can* control is how you choose to respond to these thoughts. Once you have worked through the Worry Control Blueprint—and reached the step of 'Then stop worrying about it!'—it's time to stop giving that thought any more attention. The most effective way to do this is to turn your attention to something else.

REFOCUS YOUR ATTENTION

There is always something else to turn your attention to. In most cases your worry will have intruded when you were trying to do something else: work, study, read or watch television, for example. In these cases, simply 'drop' the worry and refocus your attention on the task at hand. At other times you might be working around the house, or perhaps going for a walk. Even in these situations there is plenty else to focus on. If you're working around the house you can pay attention to whatever you happen to be doing. Many people like to have the radio or television on in the background when they do housework; if this is the case for you, focus on whatever program is on. Pay attention to what is being said or the music that's playing. Alternatively, you could choose to think about something else entirely, such as compiling your shopping list or deciding what to have for your next meal.

Just as in the case of nail biting, it's important to drop the worry immediately. Don't let yourself think about it 'just a little longer' or 'just until I find a solution' or 'just until I feel less anxious about it'. Remember that you have already established that the worry habit is not helpful and, in fact, is often harmful to your enjoyment of life if not your wellbeing. If you are to train yourself effectively not to worry, you need to learn to let go quickly and move on to more useful thoughts.

Letting go of worry has much in common with the basic concepts of meditation. An analogy from meditation likens our thoughts to so many monkeys swinging through the trees. The goal in meditation is to 'still the monkeys'. You can see that this process is a kind of mental gymnastics, which is why it is harder than inhibiting a physical behaviour. However, thousands of years of the meditative tradition have demonstrated that it is possible to master this skill with practice.

It takes most people a few days to develop the technique of letting go and refocusing. It can be frustrating when you don't quite understand how to do it, or aren't quite sure how it should feel. Stay calm, and keep trying. Many skills that require a certain 'feel' take some time to acquire. An example from my medical training was learning to use a foetal stethoscope. This was the traditional, low-tech way to listen to the heartbeat of a foetus. The foetal stethoscope was a plastic device about 20 centimetres long, shaped like a trumpet. The wide end was placed on the abdomen of a pregnant woman. The doctor's ear was applied firmly to the other end. Many, many times I listened and could hear absolutely nothing, despite doing it exactly as the professor had shown me. Then, suddenly, one day I could hear a baby's heartbeat. I guess my brain had finally worked out what I was supposed to be listening for, and had learned to distinguish it from all the background noise. After that day I never had any trouble hearing the foetal heartbeat again.

Strategies that can help to refocus

It can be helpful to give yourself a prompt to refocus. For example, you might remind yourself of the summary statement you created at the end of your cognitive challenging exercise. If Tracey finds herself starting to worry about her husband again she can say to herself, 'I've been through this. He's probably just held up.' She should take it no further, but instead refocus her attention on whatever she was doing when she began to worry. If Nick finds himself worrying again about having made a mistake he could say to himself, 'It's not likely', and then refocus his attention on the task at hand. An even more powerful response would be to say, 'Well, I'll just have to wait and see.'

Some people find it easier to use mental imagery to help them let go of thoughts and worries. Imagine 'stilling the monkeys', for example. Other people find it helpful to imagine themself holding up a stop sign. For most people, however, mental imagery is not required—all you have to do is shift your attention onto something else.

Refocusing your attention at night

It can be difficult to refocus when you are lying in bed at night trying to go to sleep. During the day, as noted above, you are almost always engaged in doing something else when the worry occurs, and so the appropriate object for your attention is right there in front of you. At night, ideally, we do not bring tasks with us to bed. As you will see later in the chapter entitled 'Better sleep', it is recommended that we don't read, watch television or worry about our problems in bed. In fact, if you want to sleep well it's essential that you train yourself not to worry. Any readers who are skilled at meditation may already be able to empty their mind of all thoughts. This is ideal, and illustrates why meditation can be so helpful for worriers. However, without training and considerable practice it is very difficult to think of nothing at all. And, as we've said, you don't have a task at hand on which to refocus your attention.

My advice in this situation is to choose a topic to think about. Ideally, this should be something that will engage your attention, but not be too stimulating or exciting, since you are trying to drift off to sleep. You should definitely not choose a problem to think about! Something pleasant and mildly interesting is ideal. The following suggestions have been found to be useful by my patients:

- Imagine how you'd redecorate your house if money were no object.
- Imagine how you'd like to restore your favourite old car.
- Think about what you'd do if you won the lottery.
- Compile your shopping list.

I never thought counting sheep was very helpful, and research has recently confirmed this view. It is so boring a task that your mind constantly wanders. In your case, this might be back into the arms of your worries, which is not what you want to happen at all. You will also notice from the above list that there is no mention of planning your workday or mulling over problem issues. Keep it light, pleasant in tone and interesting enough to engage your attention. If your mind wanders back to your worries, gently let go of them as soon as you realise what's happening, and go back to your pleasant thoughts. Be consistent at night just as you are during the day. If worrying in bed is a strong habit it may take you a week or so to improve it, and a little longer to break it entirely.

Exercises to improve your attention-focusing ability

You can improve your ability to focus your attention with practice. Have you ever noticed those people who seem to be able to put their nose in a book or glue their eyes to the television and remain oblivious to the noisy chaos of life around them? 'Yes, my husband/wife!' some of you may say. This ability to be completely focused on one thing while excluding awareness of another is particularly highly developed by some adepts in meditation. Recent experiments have measured brainwave patterns in monks who are meditating. During the experiment a loud noise is sounded nearby. Normally, the brainwaves would change, indicating that the brain has heard the noise and is processing it to determine its meaning and significance. In the case of the meditating monk, there is no indication that the noise has even been heard. This is really quite extraordinary given that hearing is not something that we can consciously turn on and off.

From this discussion it will be apparent that meditation is likely to be a helpful strategy to you, and I would encourage you to consider it as part of your long-term anxiety management plan. However, in the early stages of treatment I think it is a better investment of your energy to practise the strategies outlined in this book. These include some simple techniques for enhancing your ability to focus your attention on something of your own choosing, rather than allowing it to be hijacked by worries.

The simplest strategy is one that you can do at the same time as practising progressive muscular relaxation. All you need to do is try to keep your attention focused on what you can feel as you tense and relax your muscles. If you are using a tape or CD with recorded instructions to relax, this will give you something else to stay focused on. Inevitably, your mind will wander. As soon as you become aware that this has happened, calmly 'drop' the thought and refocus your attention on your muscles and either the spoken instructions or your own mental instructions for going through the relaxation steps. Don't get frustrated or upset, just gently let go and refocus. Be consistent—let go of any worries or distractions every time. With continued practice you will find it easier to do.

To strengthen your attention-focusing ability, you can add some distracting noise in the background. You then train yourself to ignore it and keep your attention focused on your relaxation exercises. Start with distractions that will be relatively easy to ignore and then gradually increase their level of intrusiveness. For example, you could try the following steps:

- a classical music CD playing quietly in the background
- a pop music CD playing quietly in the background
- a classical CD playing gradually more loudly
- pop music playing gradually more loudly
- having a music radio station on in the background (this will give you periods of music interspersed with talking and advertisements, which are harder to ignore than just music)
- having talkback radio or the television on in the background (you can gradually increase the volume).

Other exercises you can practise include the following:

- Select a piece of classical music. Choose one instrument to follow and see if you can focus on only this instrument as the music plays. Try this for just five or ten minutes to start with; then see if you can gradually increase the length of time for which you can do it.

- When you're walking down the street, try to keep a mental tally of how many each of red, white and blue cars you see. ('That's two red, five white and two blue; now it's three red, five white and two blue.') This is a particularly useful strategy if you tend to scan your environment for threats (for example, looking to see whether people around you look sick if you have excessive health anxiety).

FACE THE DOUBT

Always face your fears first, then move on. Confront your fears. Remember that they are only thoughts. A thought has no power to make anything happen. A thought can't hurt you. A thought has no particular significance of its own. What is important is how you react to a thought and what you choose to do about it. If this type of thinking is a problem for you, go back and re-read the section on magical thinking on page 78. Cognitive challenging will help you to be realistic about the real likelihood of a feared event. It will also help you to be realistic about how bad it would really be, and your ability to cope.

Some people think they have to keep themselves constantly busy in order to keep the worries at bay. By learning to control your worries rather than having them control you, this will not be necessary. The technique that you are aiming for is to face the fear but choose not to engage in worry about it.

Similarly, don't run away from your thoughts. Don't think to yourself, 'I can't think about that. Whatever I do, I mustn't think that thought.' Research has shown conclusively that the more we try *not* to think something, the more we experience that thought! Remember the example of trying *not* to imagine a blue elephant dancing in a pink tutu and holding a little yellow umbrella? Most people immediately visualise this very image! Ultimately, you will have much more control by allowing yourself to acknowledge your thoughts and worries—or 'face the fear'—but then take control of how you respond to them. You can choose to apply worry control strategies and then focus your attention on something more helpful to you. You can choose not to engage in worry.

By facing the fear I also mean facing the doubt about whether everything will be okay. Or, put another way, it's about facing the possibility that things could go wrong—but choosing to play the odds. You identify the *probability* rather than focus on the *possibility*. Remember: when you hear hoof beats, think of horses not zebras.

WAIT AND SEE

This is without doubt the most powerful worry control strategy of all. When you can say, 'Yes, that's possible. I'll just have to wait and see', you are in control of your anxiety and worry. This strategy is powerful because it is confronting the core issue in generalised anxiety and excessive worry: uncertainty. It is the intolerance of uncertainty, and the lack of effective strategies for coping with the anxiety it causes, that contributes to the development of excessive worry in the first place. Continued use of the worry habit protects you from confronting the uncertainty, but means that you continue to worry. As we have seen, the answer is to learn to tolerate uncertainty. The way to do this is to acknowledge it: 'I don't know what will happen. I will have to wait and see.'

I know that it is highly anxiety provoking to face the thought that something bad could happen. However, this anxiety will actually diminish significantly if you can stick it out and refrain from giving yourself reassurance, seeking it from others, or engaging in worry.

When a worry first occurs, your anxiety shoots up. If you can get some reassurance, your anxiety level will diminish quickly. If you continue to worry, your anxiety level will stay quite high. If you face the doubt and uncertainty, your anxiety level will also stay quite high—but only for a time. The length of time varies with how frightening the worst possibility seems to you, and might range from 30 minutes to two hours. Most people report that their anxiety is usually significantly less after an hour or so. If they had continued to worry their anxiety level would have remained high, although it would probably have fluctuated as the individual achieved some measure of reassurance from time to time. More importantly, they are locked into a pattern of worry and anxiety. On the other hand, the individual who begins to confront uncertainty will find that over time their level of anxiety will not peak as high and will reduce faster. Their reaction patterns will more closely come to resemble the 'normal' pattern of a person who doesn't worry excessively. They will have learned to tolerate uncertainty.

If you feel you need a quick reminder of your cognitive challenging to begin confronting your worries, that's a great start. Aim to graduate to being able to say to yourself, 'Wait and see.'

RESIST THE URGE FOR REASSURANCE

It is essential to resist the urge to reassure yourself or to seek reassurance from others. I'm not saying it's easy—just necessary. When the anxiety is severe you will feel a strong urge for reassurance. Try to see your resistance of this urge as an investment in a calmer future. If you give in now, it's like having a cigarette when you're trying to give up—it undoes a lot of your hard work and only prolongs the agony.

Be honest with yourself about sneaky forms of reassurance. For example, if you get really worried about making mistakes or missing things, you might find ways of getting someone else to check your work. Or you might 'casually' mention to your partner a decision you made and then look carefully to see how he or she reacts. If they don't seem to react at all you're reassured you probably haven't made a big mistake. People who worry about their health often see their doctor frequently for reassurance. By the time they come to see me they have usually had many tests and been to see a number of other specialists, with all the results pointing to anxiety as a cause of their symptoms. I explain that I won't be giving any more reassurance because they need to learn to cope with the uncertainty. Most people then try a few indirect approaches to elicit reassurance. For example, they might say, 'I've had that headache again. I'm not asking for reassurance, but it was a bit different this time, more throbbing and on the side. I suppose it's just my anxiety though?' Depending on their stage of therapy I might help them with a prompt like, 'What do you think is most likely?' If they're more advanced in their therapy then I will give them an encouraging smile but say nothing! Although it can be helpful to ask your loved ones not to reassure you, the main effort needs to come from you if you want to master your worry.

ONLY GO THROUGH THE WORRY CONTROL BLUEPRINT ONCE

If you have worked through the Worry Control Blueprint in response to a particular worry, you do not need to go through it again when that particular worry recurs. In fact, going over it again and again can turn into a subtle form of reassurance. The inevitable finish position on the Worry Control Blueprint is 'Then stop worrying about it!' When your worry recurs, ideally you can say, 'Well, I'll just have to wait and see.' If you can't go straight to this answer, you can remind yourself of the conclusions you drew in order to reach the 'Then stop worrying about it!' step the first time round. For example, you may have reached this step because you were able to recognise that your worry wasn't realistic. In this case you can say, 'That's not realistic', and refocus your attention on the task at hand. Or perhaps you decided the worry was realistic, but that nothing could be done about it. In this case you could say, 'Well, there's nothing I can do about it. I'll just have to wait and see', and then refocus your attention on the task at hand.

Alternatively, it may be a realistic problem, and when you applied structured problem solving to it you identified a potential solution. In completing the steps of structured problem solving you will have planned exactly how and when to implement your chosen solution, and when to review matters. So in this case you can say, 'Well, I am going to speak to my boss about it on Monday. There's nothing more to be done until then', and refocus your attention on the task at hand.

Note that in every case you resist the urge to engage in worry, you don't ruminate about the problem. Instead, you remind yourself that you have taken whatever control is possible, face the remaining element of uncertainty, and then give yourself a prompt to focus your attention on the task at hand.

To illustrate how this is all put together in practice, in the next chapter we will look at how some of our case studies might respond to their worries.

Troubleshooting

(P) 'I'm scared of letting go of my worry.'

(R) Some of your old beliefs about the benefits of worry may influence you to feel that by letting go of your worry something bad may happen. This is magical thinking. Another fear that people sometimes have is that by not worrying they may fail to find a solution to the problem. If you have worked through the Worry Control Blueprint, then you will have searched for possible solutions to your problems in a more effective way than all that worry would ever have achieved.

(P) 'I still need reassurance.'

(R) If you choose to reply to your worry with a brief summary of your cognitive challenging, it's important to be careful not to cross the line into reassurance. As you know from experience, reassurance only reduces your anxiety temporarily. Until you accept the uncertainty your anxiety will return again and again and you'll be likely to start worrying all over again. 'Wait and see' is the most powerful strategy for mastering worry because it helps you to train yourself to cope with uncertainty.

(P) 'The worry keeps coming back.'

(R) This is a universal experience. Your worry isn't going to stop just because you want it to. It's been there a long time and it's an entrenched habit. You can't change any habit overnight. The keys to success are consistency and persistence. It is not at all unusual for a worry to come back after only a few minutes. If you respond exactly the same way, every time it comes back, it will eventually weaken. Many individuals that I see are plagued by almost constant worry. When I ask them at the beginning of treatment to estimate the proportion of their day that they spend worrying, it is not at all unusual to hear that 60 per cent or more of it is spent worrying. When worry is this persistent it can seem a daunting task to bring it under control. However, with perseverance, symptoms can improve markedly in as little as three to seven days. If your symptoms are severe, and your worries return quickly at first, try not to get frustrated. You don't need the additional bad feelings. Just plod along and deal with each worry as it arises, and before you know it things will be better.

Chapter Thirteen

PUTTING IT ALL TOGETHER

The previous chapters have covered a great deal of material and it can be difficult to see exactly how it all fits together. In order to illustrate this we will revisit some of the individuals whose case histories were given earlier, and see how they might use the worry control strategies that have been outlined.

MATT

Matt is the 28-year-old junior executive who became extremely worried that he might have failed while waiting for the results of his MBA final exams. The more he thought about the questions, the more he became convinced that he had completely missed important pieces of information in his answer and was going to fail. He couldn't stop thinking about the terrible consequences for his future and the welfare of his family.

The first step is to express this as a 'what if …' Matt's 'what if …' quite clearly is 'What if I fail my exams?' We now feed this into the Worry Control Blueprint and follow the steps.

Firstly, Matt has to ask himself whether his fear is realistic. He is so anxious that he doesn't really know any more, so he answers, 'Not sure'. The Worry Control Blueprint directs him to apply *cognitive challenging* to his worry. He asks himself the following questions:

- What is the evidence for and against?
- What alternative explanations are there?
- How likely is the feared outcome really?
- How much do I have to let it matter?
- How do I gain by thinking this way?
- How do I lose by thinking this way?
- What would I say to someone else who was in this position?

He sets out his worries and their challenges using the A-B-C-D-E format in his workbook as shown on the opposite page.

Matt now decides that although it is possible that he could fail his exam (and therefore it is a realistic fear) it is really not very likely, and it would not be the end of the world. He is already less anxious.

He goes on to the next step of the Worry Control Blueprint, and asks himself: 'Can something be done about it?' This is an easy one to answer. The exam is over and done with. There is nothing he can do to change the outcome. He has either failed or he hasn't. Worrying will not change anything; therefore, there is no point in worrying about it. The Worry Control Blueprint directs him to 'Then stop worrying about it!'

Matt says to himself, 'I'll just have to wait and see.' He turns his attention back to whatever he was doing when the worry came to him. In this way his ability to concentrate on his job actually improves, and along with it his work performance. Not only does he suffer less anxiety, but he also stops compounding matters by performing sub-optimally at work. In the short term, Matt's worry will almost certainly return—after all, it's become a habit—so it is important that *every* time it does he reminds himself that there is nothing he can do about it and that he will just have to wait and see. Then he needs to refocus his attention.

A: Activating event or situation	B: Beliefs, thoughts or interpretation	C: Consequences, feelings	D: Dispute or challenge	E: Experiment or outcome
Waiting for results of final MBA examinations.	What if I fail? ▸ It would be humiliating and my boss will be so annoyed he will fire me. ▸ I will never get another job as good as this one. ▸ I'll be washed up at the age of 28 and I won't be able to educate my children or support my wife. All this worry is badly affecting my job performance. ▸ I'll lose my job for sure.	Anxiety 80 Guilt 70	I have no evidence that I have failed. I was able to answer every question and I finished the exam. I always worry that I have failed, but this is never the case. I was not as well prepared as I would have liked, but realistically this probably just means that I will not do as well as I would have liked. I did my best. I would not like to fail, but many people do and no one is critical of them. I would be disappointed but not humiliated. My boss would be disappointed for me, but he will know I have done my best and he is very unlikely to fire me. In the unlikely event that he did fire me, I would find another job, especially if I did get my MBA. If I did fail, I would use the time to study and sit again. I managed with a public education and so could my children. I may not be performing at my peak, but I'm not doing too badly, and if I control my worry I will do just as well as usual.	Anxiety 30 Guilt 0

Matt put these strategies into practice and found that within a few days he was much less anxious. He was also careful to address the physical aspects of his anxiety by exercising, controlling his breathing and practising progressive muscular relaxation. He once again engaged in activities he had been feeling 'too anxious' to do, like playing with his son and going out with the family on the weekend. After two weeks he felt much better, with less anxiety, less fatigue and better sleep.

ROSITA

Rosita is the 72-year-old 'born worrier'. Almost anything can become a trigger to worry—having to do anything outside her usual routine, feeling a bit unwell, having to make a decision. When Rosita's husband died three years ago, her anxiety became much worse. Suddenly, she had to deal with so many things that Frank used to take care of, like bills and her tax returns. She also worried much more about her health—what if she had a fall, or if something happened to her when she was at home alone and she couldn't get help? She just couldn't stop worrying about things.

We can now generate a list that summarises Rosita's problems (see below). Strategies from this book that will help to alleviate each problem have also been indicated. When you try this technique, it is important to list all of your problems so that you can make sure you target each of them.

(P) Problem: Too much worry (children's happiness, mistakes, health)
(R) Strategies: Worry Control Blueprint (chapter eight)
    Controlling health anxiety (chapter fourteen)

(P) Problem: Poor sleep
(R) Strategy: Sleep hygiene (chapter sixteen)

(P) Problem: Checking
(R) Strategy: Confronting fears (chapter fifteen)

(P) Problem: Reassurance seeking

(R) Strategy: Confronting fears (chapter fifteen)

(P) Problem: Avoiding activities outside the home

(R) Strategy: Confronting fears (chapter fifteen)

Rosita has a number of recurring worries. In addition, almost anything will trigger new worries. She avoids doing anything new or outside her usual routine because it makes her too anxious and worried. She is really quite disabled. Rosita will need to use the Worry Control Blueprint frequently.

Let's look at one of her worries: that something might happen to her when she is alone at home. As always, it's important to express the worry specifically and in detail: 'What if I fall and injure myself and can't call for help?' might be one example. Rosita can now enter this worry into the Worry Control Blueprint.

Rosita first asks herself if her worry is realistic. She sees her fear as quite realistic, especially as she gets older and more frail, and so she is directed to the next question, 'Can something be done about it?' This, too, Rosita has no trouble answering—in fact, her children have been asking her for some time to have a home monitor installed so that she can keep a 'panic button' on her that could be pressed in the event of an accident. If this idea had not already been suggested to Rosita, she would have answered, 'Not sure', and the blueprint would have directed her to do a structured problem solving exercise on the problem. If it turns out that the system the children have in mind is too expensive, then Rosita can also return to the problem and go through the steps of structured problem solving.

If Rosita chooses to go ahead with the monitoring system it would be helpful to implement her decision as soon as possible. Otherwise, a skilled worrier like Rosita might start to worry about the decision itself, for example, that the monitoring system would fail, or that she might not be able to use it when she needed to. In this case she could either feed the new worries through the Worry Control Blueprint, or alternatively—and this would be my recommendation to Rosita—she could follow Nike's advice and 'Just do it!' In other words, it would be most helpful for Rosita to focus her attention and energy on implementing the plan she has, rather than going off on a tangent with new worries. Rosita can't eliminate all uncertainty from her life. True, she could make a mistake, but she has to face this possibility and take action in spite of it—just like we all do.

Just do it!

This slogan, used by Nike to promote their shoe wear, captures an important principle. Many people defer the pursuit of their goals, waiting for more inspiration, more time, more skill, more confidence—you name it. Often what we're really frightened of is failure or lack of perfection. 'Just do it!' helps us remember that any effort is better than no effort, and that we can feel pleasure and gain a sense of achievement from even less than perfect performances.

For excessive worriers, 'Just do it!' can be a reminder that it is usually not possible to achieve complete certainty and eliminate all doubt and all possibility of harm. Sometimes we have to 'Just do it!' or life will pass us by. Sometimes we need to take risks and try things in spite of the possibility of harm or failure. If we wait for certainty we may never take a step forward at all, since we usually will not have the luxury of certainty. So once you've taken reasonable steps to reduce your risks, and you've carefully considered your options—using all the information you have available to you at the time—and made the best decision possible, it's time to 'Just do it!'

STAN

Stan is 55 and in a job he doesn't much like. He is paralysed with indecision about taking a job redundancy offer. Stan spoke to his family and friends, who gave him many conflicting opinions. The pros and cons went round and round in his head without resolving themselves. As the deadline approached he became increasingly distressed. He simply could not make a decision.

The first step for Stan in applying the Worry Control Blueprint is to identify a specific worry. On the surface of it, Stan's worry seems to be, 'What if I make the wrong decision?' But is this his real fear?

The real issue for Stan was about having enough money for his retirement. He knew he didn't like his job, but he was scared that if he took the redundancy package he and his wife might not have 'enough money'. So Stan's real fear (expressed as a 'what if …') became: 'What if we don't have enough money for our retirement?' As usual, the first step of the Worry Control Blueprint was to ask, 'Is it realistic?'. Stan thought it was, but he acknowledged that he had become so distraught with worry that he really couldn't tell any more, so he answered, 'Not sure'. He was then directed by the blueprint to use *cognitive challenging* on his worry.

He asked himself the following questions:

- What is the evidence for and against?
- What alternative explanations are there?
- What is the worst thing that could happen?
- How likely is the feared outcome really?
- How much do I have to let it matter?
- How do I gain by thinking this way?
- How do I lose by thinking this way?
- What would I tell someone else in this position?

Stan set his cognitive challenging exercise out in his workbook, using the A-B-C-D-E format. I have summarised one challenging exercise based on his worry about having enough money, showing the results of his challenges.

Firstly, the evidence for and against. Would Stan have 'enough' money? What is enough? Stan had already spoken to his accountant. His accountant felt he would have enough. This might have been satisfactory evidence for some people, but it clearly hadn't relieved Stan's fears. It would either be best for Stan to ask his accountant to take him slowly through all the calculations he'd made in reaching his opinion, or for Stan to sit down and go through it himself. Using the information his accountant had already provided as a back-up, he could make some rough estimates himself without needing a degree in economics or accounting. He could analyse his average yearly expenses, multiply this by a generous life expectancy and incorporate a component for inflation. Against this he could put the income he might expect from superannuation and his redundancy payout.

When he did this exercise Stan realised that he had to make a lot of assumptions. He had to make a guess about the rate of inflation. He had to estimate how long he and his wife might live, how long she might continue to work and whether he would find another job. He had no idea what the government pension might be in the long term, or whether taxation rates might change. No one could answer these questions. He had to accept that there were uncertainties that could not be eliminated. The only *facts* he had were that he really disliked his job and, as he realised, their expenses were really quite modest.

What were the alternatives? Stan had his accountant's advice that he and his wife would have enough money to continue their current lifestyle. This alternative had the strength of having been suggested by a trained professional in the area, and therefore, Stan realised, ought to carry some weight. Against this was his fear of not having enough—not based on any facts, just emotion. Stan needed to be careful to avoid falling into the trap of emotional reasoning.

Next Stan asked himself, 'What's the worst that could happen?' He realised that he didn't have any clear ideas of what he was afraid of. He didn't really think that they'd starve; at the very least they'd have the government pension. And he wasn't worried they'd end up on the street, because they owned their own home. He also knew that there was no way his children would let either of those things happen to them. So what was he so afraid of? He talked it over with his wife: 'I guess I'm afraid that we would have to count every penny and think carefully about even the smallest purchases before we made them.'

'Well,' his wife answered, 'we had to do that before when the children were little and I wasn't able to work. I wouldn't much like to go back to those days either, but it wouldn't be the end of the world. Is another ten years in a job you hate really worth it when Bill thinks we'd be okay anyway? I enjoy my job and I don't mind continuing to work for a while. And anyway, you might find something else.'

Stan realised the worst that could happen was not so terrible—it was certainly not ideal, but not the end of the world. He was then able to ask himself, 'How much do I have to let it matter?' He realised that he and his wife could enjoy life even if they had less money than they had become used to. If necessary they could move to a smaller, cheaper home, and perhaps make other fairly painless economies. They could manage!

Stan asked himself about gaining and losing through his pattern of thinking. He realised that by continuing to worry about his decision he could avoid actually having to make it. In a way, he could let fate decide for him, by missing the deadline to apply for the redundancy package, for example. Then it might feel that whatever happened wasn't really his responsibility. This is a common strategy employed by worriers to avoid making decisions that they feel are associated with the risk of being held responsible in the event of a bad outcome. On the minus side, Stan acknowledged that his current thinking was keeping him constantly anxious. By not making a decision he may have avoided responsibility, but he was also missing the opportunity to take control of his own destiny. In reality, it is unlikely that 'fate' will do a better job than you will if you face your fears, get the information you need and make an informed decision.

Stan decided that his advice to someone else would be to weigh up the pros and cons. He would tell them that there was no way to know for sure what the ideal solution was without a crystal ball, and they could only do their best.

After his cognitive challenging exercise, Stan decided that there was a basis in reality to his fears, but he knew that he had been overreacting. He had been reacting as if he faced a terrible catastrophe, when in fact the worst thing that could happen was uncomfortable rather than awful. He decided on balance his worries were not realistic. He decided to stop worrying about it. He also decided to use structured problem solving to help him examine his options and make the best decision he could. He recognised that this would be the one that balanced his desire for a comfortable retirement with his discomfort in his current job. Neither situation was dire.

Stan incorporated the suggestions of his accountant, his wife, children, friends and colleagues in his structured problem solving. He identified the problem as being whether to accept the redundancy package. In brainstorming he identified the following possible solutions:

1. take the redundancy package
2. don't take the redundancy package (keep the current job)
3. look for a new job.

Stan weighed up the pros and cons as follows:

Solution one: take the redundancy package

Pros	Cons
I can soon leave a job I don't like. ***	I may not find another job. **
The package is quite generous. ***	It might not make up for another ten years of work. *

Solution two: don't take the redundancy package

Pros	Cons
I could keep working and build up more super. **	I really dislike the job. ***
I might be offered another redundancy package when they downsize again. *	They might not offer the package again. **

Solution three: look for another job

Pros	Cons
I don't mind working per se. ***	Not many jobs out there. **
If I found another job it would top up my super. ***	
Maybe I could work for myself. *	

Stan decided that he could combine solution three with either solution one or two but, when he added up all the stars, the combination of one and three looked the best. He decided on these two solutions, and went ahead to plan how he would implement them.

ONCE YOU'VE MADE YOUR DECISION

It is very important that once you have completed a structured problem solving exercise, made your decision and planned how to implement it, you do not allow yourself to mull over the problem any further. Those 'what ifs' *will* come back because they are such a habit, so be prepared. Be disciplined with yourself and do not allow yourself to engage in further rumination that is now pointless. Don't accept the invitation to dance with your worry! You've made the best decision you can on the facts available. No amount of further worry will eliminate the uncertainty that inevitably remains. Face the doubt, refocus your attention on the task at hand, and move on with your life. There will be many times when we must make decisions and take action in spite of our anxiety. Remember that the anxiety is the result of the uncertainty, not evidence that you must have made a wrong decision.

Chapter Fourteen

DEALING WITH HEALTH ANXIETIES

Anxiety about health seems to be on the increase. Preventive medicine receives understandable publicity and we all want to do what we can to stay fit and healthy for as long as possible. However, for some people concern over their health passes the point of reasonableness and becomes an obsession. Over recent years I have seen an increasing number of people who are tortured by fears of ill health. They worry so much about the possibility of illness and even death that they can't relax. The slightest change in the usual 'feel' of their body can trigger panic that they may have cancer, heart disease, stroke or a serious infection. An unusual thought or the inability to control worries may lead to fear of insanity. Some people cannot bear to go out in public because they fear catching some illness from another person. They constantly scan people they come across for signs of illness. Anyone who looks in the least unwell can trigger hours or even days of anxiety as they wait to see whether they have caught something. Still others worry about the health of loved ones and rush their children to the doctor with a fever or sore throat to be sure they don't have meningitis or leukaemia. You can call this type of worry illness phobia, or severe health anxiety. At times it might qualify for a diagnosis of hypochondria.

As yet we don't know why some people and not others develop these fears. Some of my patients were exposed as children to serious illness in parents or close relatives, which might have sensitised them. Some suffered an illness themselves, which was potentially life threatening, or which was particularly frightening or unpleasant. It has been suggested that a person is more likely to develop an anxiety disorder following some frightening event if the event was completely unexpected. This type of experience has been called a 'safety violation'. In other words, you thought you were safe and then something completely unexpected happened that might have killed you. This may explain why I have seen a number of relatively young men and women who developed severe anxiety following unexpected serious illnesses such as strokes, heart attacks and blood clots. We do not expect to develop these conditions when we are young or even middle aged, particularly if we pride ourselves on living a healthy lifestyle. When it does happen it is a shocking experience that shakes our confidence in our body. When an illness experience such as this has triggered the anxiety, the individual is often fearful of having the same thing happen again, and may tend to become hypervigilant for signs of the illness recurring.

However, it is not necessary to have had a serious illness to worry excessively about getting one in the future. Another interesting observation I have made is that illness fears often seem to worsen or even develop for the first time in women after they have had children. When I have explored this, it seems for some women that they worry about getting sick or dying and leaving their children motherless.

Some people with severe health anxiety always worry about the same illness—like cancer, AIDS, meningitis, heart attack or stroke. For others the illness they fear may change from time to time. It might depend on what they have heard about recently in the news media or from relatives. Some people only worry about illnesses that might be fatal, or severely disabling, while others worry about common illnesses such as gastroenteritis and colds. They may feel that they couldn't stand to be ill, even for a short time. Some people simply can't stand the thought of particular symptoms, like vomiting. Others worry about getting sick and missing out on activities or events.

If you are feeling very anxious reading about any of this, it's a good bet that you have excessive health anxiety. Instead of skipping this chapter it is time to face your fear and try to overcome it.

BEHAVIOUR PATTERNS WHICH REINFORCE HEALTH ANXIETY

Many individuals who worry excessively about getting sick will try to avoid situations that they feel are associated with contagious elements—sick people, toxins or contamination of some sort. They may try to avoid coming across others who look ill or who they know have recently been ill. Many people who worry about illnesses like gastroenteritis may only eat certain foods. They might avoid eating out at all, or only eat at places they feel are 'safe'. Some people will always eat what their partner is eating, feeling that they would neither eat something that was 'off' nor worry excessively. This has a kind of built-in reassurance factor while also incorporating avoidance.

Some individuals who suffer from health anxiety prefer to avoid any reminder of illness. They will try to avoid reading about illness or coming across news stories about it, particularly the illness they are most sensitive about. Other people do the exact opposite. They will try to find out as much as they can about their feared illness. They may search the Internet or look up medical texts, comparing their symptoms with those they read about. Perhaps surprisingly, both of these seemingly opposite behaviour patterns serve to reinforce the individual's fears. Avoiding any reminder of the feared illness blows it out of proportion in the sufferer's mind, thereby increasing the fear. Finding out too much about it results in hypervigilance and the risk of misinterpretation (of the true benign cause of symptoms that may be on the list for that illness), and generally increases awareness of symptoms, which in turn leads to increased anxiety. Researching symptoms sometimes also acts as a kind of reassurance when the symptoms clearly do not match.

As with other types of excessive worry, reassurance seeking only strengthens the fear. Many people make unnecessary trips to the doctor, sometimes trying to disguise the true reason for the visit. They may, for example, present a child for a check-up when they are really worried about themselves. Other people ask their friends or family for reassurance. 'Did that man look okay to you?' they might ask if someone walks past them whom they fear looks ill. 'Do you think I look sick?' they might ask if they feel a bit unwell. 'Did that food taste all right to you?' they might check while at a restaurant.

Another pattern of behaviour that has the unfortunate consequence of reinforcing anxiety is excessive symptom monitoring. Earlier, we discussed the concept of hypervigilance—excessive monitoring of the external environment for signs of threat. We monitor our internal environment, too. Our brain is quietly monitoring a whole range of internal sensations. For the most part it responds to the information received according to programs that are 'hardwired' into the deepest, developmentally oldest part of our brain. Their goal is to maintain the health and safety of the body, with all systems functioning optimally. This system is also known as homeostasis and results in the management of temperature, respiration, heartbeat, blood pressure, digestion and elimination of waste. We will be alerted when we are hungry, tired or cold, or when we need to empty our bladder and bowels. Normally, this monitoring is outside of our awareness. However, if we choose to focus on these functions, it is possible to become aware of them. In some cases, it is possible to override the programs we were issued with and write new programs that direct the brain to interpret and respond differently to particular sensations. It is also possible to become aware of sensations that we would normally not notice.

There are some common examples that illustrate how focusing too much on some bodily functions can cause confusion or even create symptoms. For example, if we find ourselves in an unusually quiet situation we may hear noises in our ears that we weren't previously aware of. If we are in total darkness we may seem to see lights in front of our eyes. Another common example is suddenly feeling itchy when someone talks about having had a rash, or when your neighbour tells you her children have head lice!

When people become concerned about particular illnesses, they naturally begin to look out for symptoms. Initially, this makes sense. If you have just had an operation, it is sensible to keep an eye on how your wound is healing, and to be sure that your symptoms have gone or are diminishing, and that no new symptoms have emerged that might suggest complications. But if you continued this monitoring well after the time your surgeon expected symptoms to have resolved it would not be normal.

It's the same after many illnesses. When a person has a heart attack they will usually be given a rehabilitation program with clear guidelines for a gradual return to physical activity. It is reasonable in the early weeks of recovery to pay attention to the messages the body is giving, and to be alert for any return of pain, or any unusual physical symptoms such as breathlessness. It is wise to report these to the doctor straight away. Some people become so anxious about having another heart attack that they are reluctant to carry out any physical activity at all. They closely monitor all physical sensations to the point where they often become confused about what is normal and what isn't. If they feel a little out of breath after climbing the stairs, is it normal or not? Is it just the result of being unfit or could it be a danger signal? Similarly, they become aware of their heartbeat; perhaps noticing it is a little faster than usual. Is it normal? Should they call the doctor? Because they are so intent on catching any sign of another heart attack as soon as possible, they may worry about even mild aches or pains. For example, it is not uncommon for all of us to experience the odd muscle pain from time to time. We may never know what has caused it, and if we're not particularly anxious about our health we will probably just ignore it. But if we were really worried about a heart attack, experiencing an odd sort of chest discomfort could certainly make us anxious.

A further problem is that once we focus on a symptom it often seems to become more intense. This is particularly true for a faster heartbeat. If we feel anxious we will release adrenaline through the flight or fight response, and the inevitable physiological effect of adrenaline is to cause the heart to beat stronger and faster. This may have the effect of increasing a person's anxiety as they notice the symptom seeming to worsen.

A number of strategies are necessary to overcome excessive health anxiety. To illustrate these, let's go back to Jenny, who was introduced on page 31.

JENNY

Jenny is the 37-year-old nurse who is extremely anxious that her frequent headaches may be an undiagnosed brain tumour, despite numerous tests and visits to doctors and specialists. When she gets a headache she can't help worrying that maybe this time it really is a tumour. She carefully monitors her symptoms and tries to compare them with the last episode: are they worse this time? She thinks about the patients with brain tumours that she nursed over the years during her work. How had they presented? Did she have any of the features that they did? She often thought about the cases of young women especially, even though there were really not many of these. She wanted to read up everything she could about brain tumours, but intuitively realised this would only make her more anxious, so she resisted the urge. Despite all the medical tests, Jenny could not overcome her worries. She became constantly anxious and distressed. She began to feel tired and unwell, and saw this as further evidence of having a tumour. She also saw her anxiety as evidence of being unwell—'I feel so anxious there must be something wrong.' Her family doctor, whom she trusted, suggested that the real problem was not a brain tumour, but being unable to control her worry about the headaches.

Jenny drew up the following list of problems. Again, the strategies she could use to combat these problems have also been included.

(P) Problem: Unrealistic worry about having a brain tumour
(R) Strategies: Worry Control Blueprint
Controlling health anxiety (this chapter)

(P) Problem: Reassurance seeking
(R) Strategies: Confronting feared situations (chapter fifteen)
Confronting uncertainty (chapters seven, twelve, fourteen and fifteen)

(P) Problem: Symptom monitoring
(R) Strategies: Confronting fears (chapter fifteen)
Attention refocusing (chapters twelve to fourteen)
Worry Control Blueprint

(P) Problem: Tired
(R) Strategy: Sleep hygiene (chapter sixteen)

(P) Problem: Constant anxiety
(R) Strategies: De-arousal strategies (chapter five)

Jenny's case is typical in terms of the severity of anxiety that can be experienced by those with health anxiety. The specific concern might vary, as we have discussed above, but the anxiety is intense no matter what illness is feared. Her case also illustrates how the worry itself can be the cause of physical symptoms that may then be mistaken for symptoms of a physical illness. She also demonstrates the magical thinking that leads sufferers to interpret anxiety as being proof that something must be wrong. They think, 'There must be something wrong that has made me anxious', when the reality is, 'My fear of something being wrong is making me anxious.' It's a crucial difference to keep in mind.

Jenny demonstrates many typical features of excessive health anxiety:

- overestimated likelihood of having a serious illness
- search for reassurance, but
- failure to be reassured
- symptom monitoring
- urge to find out as much as possible about the feared condition
- misinterpretation of the true cause of her anxiety.

Jenny can get started right away with physical strategies to reduce her anxiety and arousal. If she is not sleeping well, she can apply the principles in the 'Better sleep' chapter.

The next step in managing excessive health anxiety is the same as for any type of worry: feed it through the Worry Control Blueprint. Jenny has identified the following worries:

- What if my headache is a brain tumour?
- What if the doctors are wrong and I really do have a tumour?
- What if the MRI missed something?

Let's look at her first worry: 'What if my headache is a brain tumour?' Is this a realistic worry? The very first time Jenny had this worry, it would have been understandable for her to believe that it was realistic, although it would be hoped that she would have recognised it as an unlikely possibility. Now that she has had so many tests, and second and even third opinions, it is to be hoped that she could recognise the worry as not realistic. However, it would be typical of many people who suffer with excessive health anxiety to only be able to go so far as to say they were 'not sure' if their fears were realistic or not. The next step according to the Worry Control Blueprint would then be to apply the cognitive challenging questions. Jenny's cognitive challenging of this worry is shown in Chapter 11, on page 152.

As usual, I asked Jenny to summarise the main challenges that she identified. Her summary was: 'It is extremely unlikely that my headaches are caused by a brain tumour. It is most likely that they are tension headaches, migraines or caused by too much worry.'

She was therefore able to recognise that the fear that her headache was a brain tumour was not realistic. According to the Worry Control Blueprint, her next challenge was to stop worrying about it. This meant that every time Jenny's fear came back, she needed to resist the urge to think about all the implications of possibly having a brain tumour. She needed to refuse to even consider the possibility and instead to refocus her attention on the task at hand. Initially, Jenny found this very difficult to do. I suggested that when the worry came back she could remind herself of the summary she had made following her cognitive challenging. That is, she could say to herself, 'It is extremely unlikely that my headaches are caused by a brain tumour. It is most likely that they are tension headaches, migraines or caused by too much worry', and then immediately return her attention to whatever she was busy doing at the time the fear came.

However, Jenny needed to do more than just control her thoughts in order to gain control over her worry. She needed to change her behaviour, too. On page 58 it was noted that anxiety has three main types of symptoms—physical, psychological and behavioural—and that each of these areas must be targeted to effect recovery. Hence Jenny needs to practise breathing control and relaxation techniques, as well as ensure that she gets regular exercise and adequate rest. The cognitive strategies above are directed towards her psychological symptoms. Finally, Jenny needs to tackle any behaviours that are reinforcing her worry. As noted above, Jenny constantly monitors her symptoms and also frequently seeks reassurance.

THE IMPORTANCE OF ELIMINATING SYMPTOM MONITORING

Most people have had the experience of a sore tongue, mouth ulcer, or newly filled or capped tooth. What do you remember about this experience? Most of us constantly feel the affected area with our tongue. It's as if we can't leave it alone. Does this make us more or less aware of the change? Similarly, when we notice a lump or bump or even a pimple, we keep touching it and checking it. Not only does this make us more aware of it (the pimple feels *huge* to us) but it often makes it worse! Many of my patients who worried about rashes or lumps were poking and prodding themselves as often as every few minutes. Even if you had nothing there to start with, constantly rubbing or prodding an area would soon make it sore and red! This could easily 'prove' that there was something wrong. Hence, there are several consequences of excessive monitoring of symptoms:

- Attention is constantly focused on the symptom thus making the sensation more intense.

- The constant focus of attention also makes the symptom much more prominent in your consciousness.
- Frequent touching or rubbing of any obvious physical symptom may make it more obvious—more red, tender or swollen, for example.

The aim is to be able to deal with physical symptoms in the same way that people do who are not troubled by excessive worry. Let's look at an example of how a 'normal' individual would respond to having a headache. At some point they become aware they have a headache. They might think something like, 'Oh. I've got a bit of a headache.' They wouldn't be anxious, they would simply make an observation and state it as a fact. Typically, they would then make some attempt to gauge the severity of the headache and decide whether or not to take a headache tablet. They would then act on whatever decision was made—take the tablet or not—before immediately continuing with whatever they were doing when they noticed the headache. They would *not* check its progress every five minutes: 'How's that headache now? Is it better or worse than it was five minutes ago?' They would probably not even think much about why they had a headache, or if they did, the most likely cause would not be judged to be a brain tumour. They would almost certainly attribute it to a more realistic and likely cause: tension, tiredness, a hangover, a cold. Most likely they would carry on with their activity, and perhaps several hours later might think, 'Oh. That headache's gone now.' Or, if it dawned on their awareness that the headache was still there, they would reassess whether to take a headache tablet. Once again they would carry out whatever action was decided upon and then refocus their attention. Those of you who are reading this and who are not particularly worried about brain tumours can probably recognise that you behave much like our non-worriers in this regard. It is typical that worriers behave quite normally in areas about which they do not worry excessively. Use this as a guide. Try to model your behaviour towards worry-inducing subjects on how you handle events and situations that do *not* cause you to worry excessively.

Monitoring of symptoms is a habit that you need to break. The main strategy for eliminating symptom monitoring is attention refocusing. This has been discussed in detail in chapter twelve.

RESIST THE URGE TO SEEK REASSURANCE

There are several problems with needing reassurance. Firstly, reassurance never lasts. If it really worked, you would only need to hear it once. But that's not the case, is it? Trying to get someone else to tell you things will be okay is doomed to fail, because deep down you know that there is no way they can be any surer than you are! Secondly, when you obtain reassurance against your fear, you are not learning to tolerate uncertainty. It's just a bandaid solution and doesn't treat the underlying problem of an intolerance of uncertainty. The only way to learn to tolerate uncertainty is to face it. This means either resisting the urge to seek reassurance or avoiding the anxiety in the first place. So Jenny is going to have to restrict her visits to doctors and resist the urge to ask loved ones for reassurance. She is already resisting the urge to look up the symptoms of brain tumours in medical texts, which is good work.

Appropriate reassurance

Is reassurance ever allowed? Yes. There is such a thing as 'appropriate reassurance'. Let us imagine that Jenny has had her fear of a brain tumour for the very first time, in response to a series of severe headaches that she experienced. It would be entirely appropriate for her to visit her doctor at this stage, and for her doctor to listen carefully to her description of her symptoms, to examine her and possibly order tests. If her doctor felt that her symptoms were very unlikely to be due to a brain tumour, then he would, of course, tell her this. It is a type of reassurance, but in this case entirely appropriate. Similarly, if he chose to do tests on the basis of her symptoms, this would also be appropriate, and when the results came back normal it would be appropriate to reassure her that she was unlikely to have a brain tumour. When a doctor orders tests purely on the basis that a patient has not accepted the results of previous tests, this may be inappropriate. I only say 'may' be, because I have a healthy respect for people knowing their own bodies and what is normal and abnormal for them. Hence, I might order further tests, and I would not hesitate to get the opinion of a specialist doctor in the area. Once a person had had all the tests that could be expected to pick up the illness in question, or if the only tests left carried significant risks, then I would suggest a compromise. At this stage, the weight of evidence is strongly *against* the feared illness. The only tests that are left carry the risk of complications, for example, a lumbar puncture, a cardiac catheter or cerebral angiography in Jenny's case. In this case the risk of a complication of the test greatly outweighs the risk that something serious has been missed and is therefore clearly the wrong way to go.

By the time this situation has arisen, the patient and the doctor are both extremely stressed, and at least one of them really needs to see me. At this stage, I usually put the argument to the patient that, given all the normal tests and specialists' opinions, the weight of evidence favours excessive worry and anxiety as the cause of their symptoms, rather than a serious illness. I ask them to try anxiety management strategies for the next two months. If they are no better after that, the case for further investigation can be reviewed. This balanced approach meets the aim of identifying a serious illness as soon as possible while taking account of the most likely cause of the symptoms.

In asking Jenny to resist her urges to go to the doctor we need to balance this against not missing a real illness should it occur. I give my patients some general guidelines about 'real' illness to help them make appropriate decisions about going to the doctor.

In general, with a significant illness:

- symptoms are severe
- symptoms will not go away if you ignore them
- symptoms will tend to get worse
- you often 'know' you are really unwell—in contrast to anxiety-induced symptoms where there is a part of you that 'knows' that your symptoms are not really serious and it is just your desire to be *sure* that leads you to want to visit the doctor.

If you have been anxious about your health for so long that you have lost your ability to make accurate judgments about the meaning of symptoms—whether they represent a 'real' illness or are being caused by your excessive health anxiety— then I suggest that your initial response should be to assume that your symptoms are being caused by anxiety, and to try to ignore them, at least for a time. Do this by refocusing your attention on the task at hand. If you are really worried, try setting yourself a time limit. For example, 'I will check it again in two hours. In the meantime I will ignore it and get on with my work.' It is very important that during this time you *do not monitor your symptoms*. You must resist the urge to check how your worrying symptoms are progressing—are they better or worse, are they different, etc. If you do catch yourself thinking about them, try immediately to 'drop' the thoughts and refocus your attention.

As you learn that the most common cause of your symptoms is indeed anxiety rather than serious illness, you may be able to extend the time between checks. Remember: when you hear hoof beats, think of horses not zebras. In other words, the most common causes of the day to day symptoms that people experience are innocuous: tension headaches, coughs and colds, arthritis, minor tummy upsets, and so forth. They are not cancer, strokes, heart attacks, exotic infections or unusual inflammatory conditions. However, it is certainly fair to say that you should see your doctor if symptoms persist.

In Jenny's case, because she was very anxious about her headaches, she started by trying to ignore them for just two hours at a time, then reassessing. She had become so anxious about the whole issue that she found it difficult to tell how bad her symptoms were, or whether they had changed in any way. I asked her to identify what she thought would be the characteristics of a headache that was due to a brain tumour, as opposed to headaches due to migraine, tension or anxiety. What would she expect to happen to each of these types of headaches after two hours of ignoring them? Jenny developed the table shown below.

	brain tumour	migraine	tension	anxiety
Severity	Mild to severe	Severe	Mild to severe	Mild to moderate
Duration	Fluctuates in severity but doesn't go away	Lasts several hours then goes away	Lasts a few hours	Comes and goes
What happens when you ignore it?	Doesn't really change	Doesn't really change	Gets better	Gets better
What happens if you relax?	Doesn't really change	Gets a bit better	Goes away	Goes away
Other features		Nausea, vomiting, blurred vision		Feel uneasy, worried, tense; muscle tension

Figure 14.1: Jenny's headache table.

Jenny learned from this that the severity of the headache would not be particularly useful to her in distinguishing a brain tumour from other causes of headache, and therefore she should not pay much attention to it. She reminded herself that a migraine would be associated with other features like nausea and blurred vision. She also realised that the main factors that could distinguish a headache due to tension or anxiety from a brain tumour would be that it would get better if it was ignored and go away with relaxation. She therefore devised the following plan for dealing with a headache:

1. Assume that it is due to tension or anxiety, since these are the most likely causes (when you hear hoof beats, think of horses not zebras).
2. Ignore it for two hours by getting on with the task at hand (attention refocusing).
3. Reassess in two hours:
   a. If it is better, ignore for another two hours.
   b. If unchanged, do progressive muscle relaxation (since it might be a tension headache).
4. Reassess in another two hours:
   a. If it is better, continue to ignore it,
   b. If it is still as severe as it originally was, contact husband to discuss.

Although the aim is to avoid reassurance seeking, in this plan there is a provision for a controlled level of more appropriate reassurance (contacting her husband), which can be progressively phased out as Jenny gets more confident in her own ability to determine whether a headache is significant or not. In practice, since Jenny's headaches, as we all know, were not due to a brain tumour, the vast majority of them improved after being ignored or after she did relaxation. By ignoring them she was automatically relaxing.

DON'T MISTAKE A POSSIBILITY
FOR A PROBABILITY

Jenny completed her Worry Control Blueprint and went away to practise all her worry management skills. We arranged that she would return for an appointment in two weeks time to see how she was getting on. I expected that Jenny would be feeling much better. I was surprised when she told me that she only felt a bit better. 'I am doing all the things that we talked about. I am doing the breathing and relaxation practice every day. I am trying not to monitor my symptoms. I resist calling Ian but I am still very worried. I just can't relax about the possibility that the headache *could* be a brain tumour'.

Without realising it, Jenny had fallen back into the trap of wanting complete certainty. She wanted to be *sure* that her headache could not be due to a brain tumour. I gently reminded Jenny that it is rarely, if ever, possible in life to have complete certainty. I reminded her that in areas of her life where she did not have excessive and unreasonable worries, she was quite capable of dealing with uncertainty. For example, Jenny and her husband had recently taken out a large mortgage to buy a new house. She had no guarantee that either she or Ian would not lose their jobs, nor that the house would prove a good investment, yet she didn't worry. 'Yes,' she said to me, 'But it's not like losing the house could kill us.'

I accepted that this was true, but pointed out that she drove her car every day without a second thought, even though it was possible that she could have an accident. 'It's not very likely ...' she replied. And that's exactly the point. In other areas of her life Jenny was as able as anyone else to deal with the uncertainties of life. In fact, it is possible that we could be killed driving our car, but most of us assess this as being highly unlikely and judge the benefits of time saving and convenience as far outweighing the risk. It is *possible* that we could die, but we accept this possibility, judge it as highly unlikely and cope by not giving it any further thought. In other words, we do not engage in constant, repetitive thinking about the risks of driving and instead get on with the task in hand. In reality, the sobering truth is that it was far more likely that Jenny would die in a car accident than from a brain tumour.

What Jenny needed to do was to accept that there simply were no guarantees about not having a brain tumour, and all that she could do was to 'play the odds'. In other words, instead of focusing on the *least likely* explanation (having a brain tumour), she should focus on the *most likely* explanation for her headaches (tension, anxiety or migraine). In the process she needed to accept that the remote possibility can not be eliminated but, like other remote possibilities of harm, she can learn to live with it. The trick is not to focus on the remote possibilities.

Jenny went away and tried to apply this way of thinking. With this new perspective, in combination with her worry management strategies, she experienced a significant reduction in anxiety.

Health anxiety checklist

If your worry and anxiety about having an illness is not diminishing as you expect, go through the following checklist:

- Are you monitoring your symptoms in some subtle way?
- Are you still focusing on the *possibility* of harm, rather than on the *probability* of safety?
- Are you asking for too much reassurance?
- Are you looking for reassurance in more subtle ways, such as by looking up information about your feared illness, taking your temperature or pulse, or checking with others who may have been exposed to similar conditions?

- Are you doing your relaxation and breathing control exercises?
- Are you leading a normal life, or are you avoiding situations that trigger your health anxiety?

Let's look now at two more examples of health anxiety so that you can practise recognising the characteristics, and learn more about implementing the appropriate management strategies.

Noah's story

Noah is a 16-year-old high school student. He has always tended to worry about things. He worries about making mistakes at school and getting in trouble with teachers, or failing his exams. He worries about whether his parents are okay when he isn't with them. He worries about whether he has said something silly when he's socialising with his friends, and worries they may think he's foolish. Noah worries about having car accidents, or burglars robbing the house. On top of all this, he also worries about his health. If he is buying takeaway food, he likes to check first that the person preparing his food looks clean and healthy, or else he will leave and get his meal somewhere else. If he has been near someone whom he thought looked ill in some way he becomes very anxious. If Noah's mother is with him when he passes the person who worried him he is likely to ask her if she thought that person looked okay. He won't ask his father because his father gets cross, and he won't ask his friends because then they would know there was something wrong with him and he worries they might think he was crazy.

He will ask his mother to check his temperature, or to say whether she thinks he looks all right. He will stay up late at night until he feels the incubation period has passed and he can safely conclude he has escaped infection. He says that if he doesn't he can't sleep anyway, he will be too anxious. Noah believes that if he is still okay six hours after he has had some worrying contact, then he won't get sick. Because he doesn't like staying up late, he tries to be home by 4 pm. This means he will rarely accept invitations to eat out in the evening, often staying home when the rest of his family go out.

In treating Noah, I wanted to know more about his symptoms, and I asked him many questions to obtain the history given above. There was still more that I needed to know to help him overcome his anxiety. What happened when he started to worry? He said he would become anxious, sweaty and unable to relax or go to sleep. He would lose his appetite and often feel sick in the stomach. Sometimes he would feel a lump in his throat, and very occasionally short of breath.

What exactly was he frightened of? It turned out that Noah's biggest fear was of getting food poisoning or gastroenteritis. He wasn't frightened that he might die, but he wasn't quite sure what he was frightened of. Noah's fears were really quite vague, and he had great difficulty pinning them down. It is often easier to identify underlying thoughts and worries when you use a specific incident of anxiety, and that is what I did with Noah. I asked him to take note of an incident where he became anxious and to come to the next session with an example.

Noah's example was that he had gone out to the local shopping mall to meet his friends on Saturday afternoon. He had been anxious about going, and had been avoiding it for some weeks, but his mother persuaded him to go. While he was there a man who looked unwell had walked quite close to him and he became very anxious. He did not stay long after that, returning home where he felt safer. I asked Noah what he had been worrying about. He replied, 'I worried that I might get sick.' After some discussion we identified that he was afraid of getting an illness that would make him vomit. I asked what worried him about vomiting, and again he had to think quite hard, but he was able to identify that he worried both about missing out on something and about perhaps not getting better.

Noah's symptoms can be divided into the three areas common to all anxiety problems:

- Psychological: fear of getting ill, fear of vomiting, fear of not getting better.
- Physical: unable to relax, insomnia, sweating, nausea, lump in throat, shortness of breath.
- Behavioural: reassurance seeking (from his mother, checking his temperature, staying up until he is sure that the 'incubation' period has passed), avoidance of situations that trigger anxiety (situations where he feels he might get sick).

I introduced Noah to the Worry Control Blueprint and encouraged him to feed his worry through the flow chart. His first impulse was to say that his fears were realistic. However, he was also aware of the fact that he worried much more than anyone else he knew about getting sick, and therefore he had to say that at the very least there could be some doubt about whether his fears were realistic. He opted for 'not sure'. He then went on to do cognitive challenging, asking himself the following questions:

- What is the evidence for and against?
- What alternative explanations are there?
- How likely is the feared outcome really?
- What's the worst that could happen?
- How much do I have to let it matter?
- How do I gain by thinking this way?
- How do I lose by thinking this way?
- What would I say to someone else in this situation?

He used the five-column format (A-B-C-D-E) and wrote it all down in his workbook, as shown on the opposite page.

Noah initially found it quite difficult to challenge his beliefs. He felt that it was highly likely that if someone sick walked close by him, he could catch something. It was therefore very appropriate for me to provide Noah with factual information about the transmission of infection: you can't get sick if you don't 'catch' the bug. This was not reassurance, but essential information. However, if I was to keep repeating it, then it could have become reassurance. (Having passed the information on to Noah, it was now up to him to apply it, and not up to me or his family to use it to reassure him.) To catch a cold, the virus responsible has to land on a suitable body surface like your nose, mouth or eyes. To catch gastroenteritis you really have to eat the bug. Although someone walking past could give you their cold if they were able to cough directly on to you, there really is no way a passing individual can transmit a gastro bug! The same holds true of other sorts of illness that people commonly worry about, like AIDS and hepatitis. You don't get them from casual contact. You don't get them from walking past blood spots or people who look like they 'might' have the illness (or even people who do have the illness, although you usually wouldn't be able to tell).

Noah wasn't sure how likely it was that he would get ill. I asked him when he had last actually had a vomiting illness. He said it was when he was nine years old, when everyone in the family got sick. I asked him to estimate how many times a week he worried about getting sick, and then to work out his ratio of actually getting sick, much in the way Tracey worked out the odds of her husband having a car accident in chapter eleven.

(P) How many times per week on average do I worry about getting sick?

(R) Five

A: Activating event or situation	B: Beliefs, thoughts or interpretation	C: Consequences, feelings		D: Dispute or challenge	E: Experiment or outcome	
A man walked close to me at the mall. He looked sick.	What if I get sick? I might vomit—that would be horrible. I might never get over it.	Anxiety Nausea Lump in throat	90 50 60	*Evidence* The man did look sick, but he might not have been. You can't really tell by looking. The doctor says you can't catch gastroenteritis just because someone sick walks past you. Most of the time when I have worried I would get sick I didn't. *Alternatives* I feel nausea and a lump in my throat because I am anxious, not because I am getting sick. *How likely?* Very unlikely. *Worst thing* Vomiting would be the worst thing, but I guess I could cope with it—I did before and other people do. *How much does it matter?* I don't have to worry about it so much. When I did get sick before, I got better in just a few days. I have heard of other people getting sick and they always get well in a few days. *Gain/lose* Thinking this way makes me anxious all the time and stops me from going out with my friends. It doesn't really help because the one time I did get sick I probably got it from my brother.	Anxiety Nausea Lump in throat	50 30 0

(P) For how many years have I worried?

(R) Six

(P) What is the total number of worry episodes?

(R) 5 x 52 (weeks) x 6 (years) = 1560

(P) How often have I actually got sick?

(R) Once

From this it was possible to calculate that so far Noah's risk of getting sick was 1/1560 or 0.06 per cent.

Based on these calculations it was clearly highly unlikely that he would get sick. It was even being generous since he probably got his illness when he was nine from his younger brother and not someone he passed in the street!

I asked Noah to summarise his conclusions for future use. He wrote: 'It is extremely unlikely that I could catch anything from someone just walking past me, and even if I did, it would not be that bad and I would get over it quickly.'

Noah concluded that his fears were unrealistic. The Worry Control Blueprint directed him to, 'Then stop worrying about it!'

However, to stop worrying about his fears, Noah will require a combination of cognitive and behavioural strategies. He will need to:

- *Stop monitoring his symptoms.* When he notices that he feels nauseated or has a lump in this throat he needs to remind himself that the most likely cause is anxiety and not gastroenteritis. (When you hear hoof beats, think of horses not zebras.) He then needs to take a 'wait and see' approach and refocus his attention on the task at hand. Either he has been exposed to a virus or, more likely, he has not. There is nothing he can do about it now, either way.

- *Resist the urge to seek reassurance.* If Noah can learn to tolerate uncertainty he will no longer be troubled by excessive anxiety. His mother cannot guarantee that he will be okay. He therefore has nothing to gain by asking her; he may feel reassured for a short period of time, but his anxiety will return. On the other hand, he has much to lose, since by constantly seeking reassurance he will not learn the essential skill of tolerating uncertainty, and he will continue to suffer unreasonable levels of anxiety. Similarly, checking his temperature will only provide temporary reassurance, and is no guarantee that he won't get ill. It will reinforce his inability to tolerate uncertainty, a normal part of life.

- *Engage in normal activities of life.* Ideally, Noah will try to live a normal life. That means doing the things he'd like to be doing, if it weren't for his anxiety: going out with his friends, eating out with friends and family, going to bed when he is tired rather than staying up until he feels he's over the danger period. It is very important that behaviour matches the rational thinking, rather than the unreasonable pattern of thinking. In this way, the *rational* way of thinking will be reinforced. Noah can apply the principles of graded exposure to confront feared situations gradually.

- *Don't respond to worry.* In other words, when a worrying thought enters his mind, it is important for Noah to resist entering into mental discussions or ruminations about it. If it is a new worry, he should feed it through the Worry Control Blueprint. If it is an old worry returning, he should hit it with the summary of his cognitive challenging or structured problem solving, then 'wait and see'.

Some people have more realistic illness worries, like Tom. Tom is the 54-year-old teacher who was introduced on page 33. He developed excessive anxiety about developing another arrhythmia after surviving an irregular heartbeat that he was told could have killed him.

In Tom's case, when he used the Worry Control Blueprint, he reasoned that his fears were quite realistic—it had happened once, and, although unlikely to happen again, it was possible.

The next step on the flow chart was to ask himself whether something could be done to reduce his risk or prevent another episode of arrhythmia. He wasn't sure, so he applied structured problem solving. He also decided to visit the cardiologist again to ask about this in more detail, and better inform his structured problem solving. The specialist congratulated him on his healthy lifestyle, and encouraged him to keep it up. It had no bearing on his having developed an arrhythmia, but would greatly reduce his risk of heart attack, high blood pressure and diabetes. All Tom's blood tests had been normal, including his blood sugar and cholesterol. Nothing needed to be done in these areas. The specialist told Tom that they really had no idea what had caused the irregular heartbeat Tom had experienced, but that the rates of recurrence had been shown to be very low. He advised Tom to stop worrying about it and lead a normal life. 'Your chances are no greater now than they were before. So you should lead your life the same way you used to'.

Tom realised that there was nothing more he could do to reduce his risk. Both his cardiologist and the Worry Control Blueprint suggested he should stop worrying about it.

But it was difficult for Tom to stop worrying. He couldn't help feeling that by worrying about it he could somehow prevent it happening. By remaining alert he could catch it early. I asked him what he thought in retrospect were the early warning signs. He replied that it was finding his runs more physically challenging than normal. We agreed that this information could be filed away for future reference, without the need for Tom to monitor his physical state as carefully as he was at present. This is similar to the way we learn to recognise other patterns in life. We don't think about them constantly but file them away for future reference. For example, in medical training doctors need to learn the clinical features of a large number of illnesses. They file this information away and rely on recognising the pattern when it occurs. Asthma sufferers need to learn to recognise an asthma attack when it occurs—but doctors don't suggest they monitor their breathing every hour of every day.

Tom also realised that his belief that he could prevent a recurrence by worrying about it was a kind of magical thinking. He was finally able to accept that there was nothing to be gained by continued worry and excessive monitoring and he agreed to begin the process of getting back to a normal life.

Whenever Tom's worry about his heart returned, he reminded himself of the conclusions he'd drawn from working through the Worry Control Blueprint: 'Worrying about it won't help. I need to get on with my life.'

Tom had become unfit. It was unreasonable and inadvisable for him to go straight into vigorous exercise, even if he hadn't still been very anxious about it. He had also developed the tendency to misinterpret any physical symptoms that resembled the symptoms of his arrhythmia as evidence that he'd developed another one—even though at another level he knew he was overreacting. So he also needed the chance to get used to the symptoms of physical exertion again (feeling warm, slightly out of breath and having a slightly raised heart rate). We decided he would start just by taking some slow walks. Our initial target was for him to walk at an easy pace for ten minutes at a time, and to do this four times a week. Over the ensuing weeks

Tom very gradually increased the duration and level of his exertion. He regained both his confidence and his fitness, although there were many times where he had to work at controlling his worry and anxiety.

Tom's case is an example of using a gradual (or graded) approach to confronting feared situations and achieving a return to normal life. As this technique can be applied to a range of fears and worries, it is covered in more detail in the next chapter.

Chapter Fifteen

CONFRONTING FEARED SITUATIONS

If worry and anxiety are to be effectively managed, it is necessary for the behavioural aspects to be addressed along with the psychological and physiological symptoms. The main behavioural changes that occur in response to excessive worry include:

- reassurance seeking
- avoidance of situations that trigger anxiety
- monitoring of symptoms or the environment (hypervigilance).

These behaviours are probably attempts to find certainty and thus alleviate anxiety. Since certainty is often unattainable no matter what efforts are made, the actual result is to reinforce an intolerance of uncertainty and perpetuate anxiety and worry.

If any of these behaviours are resisted, the person will initially feel more anxious, since they will be confronting their fear and uncertainty rather than relieving it with some illusory certainty. For example, the reassurance of another person tells us, 'It's okay.' Avoiding situations means we don't have to deal with the worry in the first place. Monitoring symptoms or the environment relieves anxiety because we can say, 'All clear.' As your own experience tells you, however, this relief of anxiety is only temporary, because reassurance *never lasts*. A colleague of mine asks his patients, 'How much reassurance would I have to give you so you never have to ask again?' Every patient knows that there is *no* amount of reassurance that would work forever.

In previous chapters there has been some illustration of graded exposure, for example, with Jenny and Tom in chapter fourteen. In this chapter the principles that underlie graded exposure will be discussed in more detail, in order to help you recognise your own need to confront feared situations and plan your own program.

GRADED EXPOSURE

Since relinquishing anxiety-relieving behaviours will initially increase anxiety, it is too difficult for most people to let go of all their behaviours at once. Instead, we use a gradual approach, known as *graded exposure*.

A graded approach, accomplished in a planned and structured way, can be used to enable someone to let go of all the behaviours noted above. Subjective Units of Distress, or SUDs, scores can be used to ensure that the resulting anxiety is not overwhelming, and that the level of exposure is increased gradually. SUDs ratings can also be used to estimate the level of anxiety that results when anxiety-provoking thoughts and situations are confronted. These estimated scores can then form the basis of a planned program to relinquish reassurance seeking and monitoring, and re-engage in normal activities.

RESISTING THE URGE FOR REASSURANCE

As we have seen, reassurance seeking can be overt or subtle. Kim, whom we met earlier on page 84, displays both forms of behaviour.

Kim, 40, worried whenever her children aged 17 and 20, were out of the home. She worried about them getting sick, being kidnapped, having accidents. She could not stop worrying until they returned home. Her children knew they had to call her as soon as they arrived where they were going, to reassure her they were safe. Kim would call them frequently while they were out to make sure they were okay. She would not go to sleep at night until they were safely home. Kim also worried about her husband's welfare. He knew to call her if he was going to be late home, or if he had to go out of the office for some reason, as she would become distraught if she tried to reach him and he was not in the office. Kim's behaviour was upsetting to her family and did not help her to worry any less.

A subtle form of reassurance seeking is Kim's insistence that her children leave their mobile phones on—she knows she can reach them at any time and get instant reassurance that they are okay. Less subtly, she has trained both her children and her husband to provide reassurance that they are safe. They do this because they do not like to see the person they all love become upset. However, by seeking and obtaining reassurance whenever she wants it, Kim has not learned how to cope with normal everyday uncertainty. The behaviours she requires of her family intrude on their lives. Along with straight thinking and application of the Worry Control Blueprint, Kim will need to learn to resist the urge to seek reassurance, and instead tolerate the uncertainty of not knowing *for sure* that her husband and children are safe as they go about their daily business.

Kim was asked to estimate the SUDs that would result if the following behaviours were *stopped*:

Behaviour	SUDs (if no action)
Children call Kim as soon as they arrive at destination:	
Youngest, daytime	70
Youngest, night-time	95
Oldest, daytime	50
Oldest, night-time	70

Behaviour	SUDs (if no action)
Kim calls children while they're out:	
Youngest, daytime	60
Youngest, night-time	100
Oldest, daytime	40
Oldest, night-time	90
Kim doesn't go to sleep until child/children safely home	100
Husband informs her if he leaves the office	50
Husband calls if he's going to be home late	80
Children keep their phones switched on	65

Generally, SUDs around 40 to 60 are considered moderately challenging, and are around the level that we recommend you begin working at. You can also start at lower levels of SUDs. Kim could begin by resisting the urge to call her oldest child during the day. Kim has rated this a 40, so we would expect her to be able to tolerate the resulting anxiety. When you rate your anxiety, it is better to overestimate the anxiety that might result, rather than underestimate, because it is a much nicer experience to find something easier than you expected, rather than much more anxiety provoking and distressing. At the same time, Kim could also relieve her husband of the requirement to phone her if he leaves the office, but he should still phone if he is going to be late (because this has a much higher rating).

In graded exposure you work at the same level until the behaviour seems reasonably easy, or the SUDs have reduced to 30 or lower. Then you choose the next most anxiety-provoking situations.

There is another way that Kim can tackle some of her behaviours. For example, she could reduce the frequency with which she calls her youngest child during the day. I asked her to monitor her usual rate of calling, and she said she would call the youngest two or three times during the day. It depended a bit on how 'dangerous' she perceived the place her child was going to be was. She could then compare the SUDs for calling only once a day, with calling twice and calling three times and then use this as a graded approach.

Noah, who was introduced on page 201 and who worries about a range of situations, could use the same technique to modify his behaviour. One of the ways in which he reassures himself is by checking things. For example, he checks his schoolwork repeatedly, and checks that the door is locked if he is the last to leave. Noah can construct a graded exposure program for himself based on these behaviours. He might find that he worries more about checking some subjects than others and this would be one way that he might be able to generate a range of SUDs levels to make his exposure graded. For example, since Noah finds geography relatively easy, it might cause him less anxiety to limit his checking of his geography homework than it would his maths homework. Similarly, there might be times he would worry more about checking the door than others. For example, if he was the last to leave and knew no one would be home all day he would worry more than if he knew someone would be home soon.

The golden rules of graded exposure

In order to effectively reduce anxiety in the long term, and increase tolerance to uncertainty, the graded exposure must be:

- *Frequent*: It's unfortunately not helpful if you only confront your fear now and again. In fact, the more frequently you confront it, the sooner you'll overcome it.
- *Repeated*: You need to do it over and over again for the anxiety to diminish.
- *Consistent*: It won't work if you confront the situation sometimes and not others, depending on how you feel. You need to confront the situation in spite of feeling anxious. This is why it can be better to overestimate

the amount of anxiety you expect, rather than underestimate. Similarly, start at the easiest level you can and work your way up. It's not a race. Consistency is more important than speed—you've probably had your anxiety for a while, a few more weeks won't hurt.

- *No escape*: It's important that once you embark on confronting a given situation you don't bail out and ask for reassurance after all or leave the situation before you planned to (like Noah did on page 202 when someone he thought looked ill walked near him).

- *Sustained*: Ideally, you continue to confront the situation until your anxiety begins to diminish. Sometimes you may plan to confront it for a set time limit—in the last chapter Jenny devised a graded exposure plan where she resisted checking her headache for two hours at a time. The time you set will be determined by a range of factors, including SUDs levels, and characteristics particular to the situation: perhaps how long it is reasonable to leave a child unsupervised or how long it is reasonable to observe a physical symptom before getting a medical review. Whatever time you set, try to stick to it.

AVOIDANCE OF SITUATIONS THAT TRIGGER ANXIETY

Noah mostly avoids eating out and going out with his friends, in case he is exposed to someone who looks ill. He needs to plan how he can return to normal everyday activities like these. Since his fear is about catching an illness, his SUDs levels will be largely determined by how great a risk he feels is posed by a given situation. However, we also know that Noah does not like to go out in the evening because he avoids going to bed unless he is sure in his own mind that he will not become ill, so this will be a factor, too. Noah's exposure hierarchy (a program which arranges graded exposure situations in order of their potential to induce anxiety) might look like this:

Situation	SUDs
Go to the cinema with friends at a quiet time of day and sit away from other people	40
Go to the Mall with friends and stay for one hour in the morning	50
Get a takeaway sandwich from a deli he has eaten from before	50
Go to the Mall with friends and stay for two hours in the morning	60
Go to the cinema for the 5 pm session	70
Have lunch at a café	70
Go to the Mall after school and stay for one hour	80
Have dinner at friends of the family	90
Eat out at a restaurant with the family for dinner	100

Noah can start with the first one or two on his list. He will need to repeat these frequently. For example, he can go to the cinema once a week and go to the Mall every day during school holidays or each day on the weekend. Ideally, he would do these activities every day, but it isn't feasible in this case. A compromise is called for. Noah will need to combine these activities with resisting reassurance-seeking behaviours such as taking his temperature and asking his Mum if people look okay to her. He will need to make a rule for himself that he goes to bed at the same time each night no matter whether he has been out or not.

Many individuals with excessive health anxiety avoid situations that remind them of illness. This includes visiting friends or relatives in hospital, watching television programs about health or illness, or reading about illness. These activities are part of life. Although the aim is certainly not to go to the opposite extreme and become focused on illness, it is reasonable to be informed about health issues. It is unreasonable to have to turn off the television or change the channel because there is some mention of illness, or to avoid visiting a sick friend because of a phobia about illness. A graded exposure approach can be devised by using SUDs. In this case, the level of anxiety might vary according to the type of illness, the setting or the type of story (fiction, documentary, news, magazine with pictures, television, friend's story and so forth).

MONITORING OF SYMPTOMS OR THE ENVIRONMENT

In chapter fourteen, as part of her treatment, Jenny was advised of the importance of not monitoring her symptoms. Many people who worry about their health are not even aware of how much attention they pay to the physical state of their body. It has become a habit in response to their anxiety. If you have excessive health anxiety, look carefully to see whether you are monitoring your physical state excessively.

What is excessive? People without health anxiety do not monitor their physical health at all. They rely on the brain to alert them to any significant change, rather than constantly checking for it. This is why I suggested to Tom that he file away information about the early warning signs of an arrhythmia, and then rely on his brain to do the rest. We often do this unconsciously in life and it works very well. An example given earlier was of the new mother who unconsciously programs her brain to alert her in response to unusual behaviour from her baby. Mothers with young babies cannot wait up like Kim or Noah until they are sure things are okay—they'd have to be awake 24 hours a day. Another system is needed, and it is supplied by nature. Write the program for yourself—what is reasonable for you to respond to—and trust your brain to do the rest.

Initially, you will have to break the habit of monitoring your internal or external environment, by catching yourself in the act and deliberately refocusing your attention. For Jenny and Tom this means not monitoring the physical symptoms they respectively fear. For Noah it means not scrutinising people he comes into contact with to see how sick they look. He developed this habit without even realising it. He has created a vague notion of what identifies a person as probably being ill without this having any factual basis at all! It is another case of magical thinking. Noah will overcome his anxiety most effectively by:

- Going out in spite of feeling anxious about it.
- Not paying any particular attention to people he comes across, and definitely not trying to make judgements about their state of health. He must 'take his chances'.
- Not monitoring his physical state once he gets home.
- Going to bed at the usual time whether he has been out or not.

YOUR GRADED EXPOSURE PROGRAM

Set your goal as being able to lead a normal life, doing the things you want to do without being limited by anxiety. Use graded exposure to help you gradually return to doing the things in life you've been avoiding.

Avoidance

Make your own list of situations you avoid, or things that you don't do as you'd like. Many people incorporate avoidance so gradually into their lives that they find it hard to list all the things they have grown to avoid. Below are some of the things that my patients have told me during treatment, when we were discussing the topic of avoidance.

- 'I don't like to commit myself to attending social functions in case I jinx myself and something bad happens.'
- 'I can't plan holidays because I get too anxious about it.'
- 'I will never volunteer to organise anything because I don't like to be responsible.'
- 'I never want to be in charge because I couldn't cope if something went wrong.'
- 'I don't like to go anywhere I haven't been before.'
- 'I don't like to drive in heavy traffic.'
- 'I don't like to drive out of my comfort zone.'
- 'I won't travel overseas.'
- 'I don't like to be too far from a doctor or hospital.'
- 'I avoid having to make decisions.'
- 'I won't look for a new job because I'm too anxious.'
- 'I don't like change.'
- 'I won't listen to the news—there might be an accident, or talk of some illness.'
- 'I can't listen to any stories about illness.'

What can you put on your list?

Avoidance behaviour	SUDs

Give each behaviour a SUDs rating, determined on the basis of how anxious you would feel if you confronted the situation or carried out the activity in question. If it would depend on specific factors, such as who was involved, how far you were travelling, what you had to do and so forth, then describe each different example and give it its own SUDs rating. For example, if your reluctance to commit to social events depended on who would be present, how formal it was and how far in advance it was, then you should be specific about each of these factors, such as:

Situation	SUDs
Informal barbecue with my family for next weekend	50
Wedding invitation—friend of husband's, six months away	90
Friend rings to ask me over for coffee next day	40
Go on roster for school canteen	100
Invited out to restaurant with friends in two week's time	80

Be specific about the situations you describe. If you can't drive outside your 'comfort zone', consider a range of driving destinations, all with different SUDs. For example, the next suburb, a shopping complex just slightly farther away than your usual one, visiting a friend or relative across town. If in doubt, overestimate how anxious you would feel, or rate it from the perspective of how you would feel at your worst (for example, on a day when you felt quite anxious and lacking in confidence). Think of the goals you would like to be able to achieve and write these down as additional exposure targets.

Reassurance seeking

You also need to list all the behaviours in which you engage to try to get reassurance. Consider the following:

- Asking a friend or loved one directly for reassurance about a worry.
- Asking someone to check something you have done.
- Asking someone if you seem well.
- Asking someone if they think you have made the right decision.

- Checking something yourself—for example, your temperature or pulse, or checking work that you have done.
- Telling yourself over and over in your head that 'there is nothing to worry about' or 'it's okay' or other mental reassurance rituals. (Note: these do not confront the fear, they avoid having to think about it.)

What are your own reassurance-seeking behaviours?

Reassurance-seeking behaviour	SUDs

For each reassurance-seeking behaviour that you identify, give a SUDs rating based on how you would feel if you *resisted the urge* to seek that reassurance. If there are different sub-types of situations where the SUDs would differ, describe these in detail.

Implementing your exposure program

Now go through both lists and identify some avoidance and/or reassurance-seeking behaviours with SUDs of around 40 to 50. These are the behaviours you will target first. Confront the avoided situation/s and resist the reassurance-seeking behaviour repeatedly and frequently until it no longer makes you very anxious. Check the SUDs it causes you by keeping a record every time you complete the exposure. When your SUDs have reduced to 30 or less consistently, you can move on to your next targets. These will either be more of your 40 to 50 SUDs or, if there are none left, move up to the next lowest-rated SUDs activities on your lists.

Make sure you also have a list of goals regarding situations or activities you would like to be able to do. Arrange these in order of increasing difficulty and incorporate these into your program.

Troubleshooting

(P)'I don't have anything with SUDs less than 70 or higher.'

(R) If this is the case, see if you can break down the challenge into smaller challenges, as we did with the driving example given above. Another way to reduce SUDs when it comes to reassurance-seeking behaviours is to impose time limits. For example, initially make yourself wait two hours before asking or checking. As you grow more confident gradually extend this period. With a bit of imagination you can usually find some way to break a hard challenge into easier steps.

(P)'The tasks are not getting any easier.'

(R) This can happen if you are still giving yourself a sneaky bit of reassurance without realising it. When I help my patients analyse what is holding them back when they don't seem to be making progress, we often find they are reassuring themselves without realising it, perhaps mentally saying, 'It's okay' or monitoring themselves. See also the discussion of Jenny's progress in chapter fourteen.

Graded exposure can certainly be hard work, but the pay off is being able to do all the things you've lost over the years because of your anxiety, and being free of the worry that keeps you dependent on reassurance.

Chapter Sixteen

BETTER SLEEP

Sleep problems are common in the general population: one recent survey estimated that 51 per cent of people had experienced insomnia in the past 12 months. Insomnia lasting two weeks or more and accompanied by significant distress or impairment is reported by a much lower proportion, in the range of 8 to 15 per cent of people according to some sources. Almost everyone with anxiety reports some problems with sleep. Some people have great difficulty falling asleep at night because they are worrying too much. Others are exhausted by spending the day worrying, and fall asleep easily, but tend to sleep restlessly and wake frequently through the night. Many anxious individuals wake anxious and unrefreshed, and quickly feel burdened by another day of worry. There may be many causes of finding sleep unrefreshing, including:

- not getting enough sleep
- irregular sleep pattern
- too many wakeful periods through the night
- anxiety starts again immediately upon waking.

Happily, there is much that can be done to improve the quality of your sleep. First and foremost, controlling your anxiety during the day is one of the most important strategies for reducing night-time anxiety. Exercise and relaxation will calm your system down and reduce arousal. Controlling your worry and anxiety during the day will reduce the 'ammunition' for worry through the night. Controlling your worry in bed at night will further assist.

Apart from these general strategies there are some specific guidelines that you can follow to enhance the quantity and quality of your sleep. The first step is to assess your current sleep pattern.

ASSESSING YOUR CURRENT PATTERN OF SLEEP

Every night for two weeks record the following information:

- The time you went to bed.
- The time you estimate you fell asleep.
- Approximate times of waking and getting back to sleep during the night.
- If you got out of bed during the night, the time you got up and the time you went back to bed, then the time you fell asleep again.
- The time you woke up in the morning.
- The time you got out of bed in the morning.

This information can be recorded quite easily by using a chart like that shown below. Use a downward arrow (↓) to indicate that you got into bed. Use an upward arrow (↑) to indicate that you got out of bed. If you were asleep, shade the box. If you were awake, leave the box blank. You can then see your sleep pattern at a glance. This chart uses the 24-hour clock in order to save space, so 13 (short for 1300 hours) is one o'clock in the afternoon, 14 (short for 1400 hours) is two o'clock in the afternoon, and so forth up to 24, which is midnight.

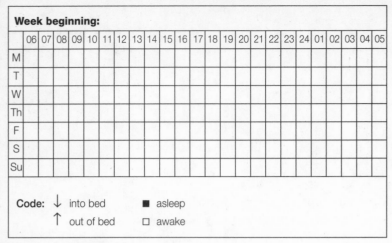

Week beginning:																								
	06	07	08	09	10	11	12	13	14	15	16	17	18	19	20	21	22	23	24	01	02	03	04	05
M																								
T																								
W																								
Th																								
F																								
S																								
Su																								

Code: ↓ into bed ■ asleep
       ↑ out of bed □ awake

Figure 16.1: Sample sleep chart

On page 85, we met Sam, 45, who had a long history of excessive worry as well as chronic insomnia. On the opposite page is one of Sam's sleep charts.

From this chart we can see that Sam awoke and got out of bed around 7 am on Monday morning. (You can make your own chart more precise by drawing your arrow towards the beginning or end of the time slot.) He went to bed at 8 pm and was asleep by about 9 pm, remaining asleep until some time around midnight when he experienced broken sleep before finding himself awake at 1 am for an hour or so. He slept again for an hour around 2 am, then lay awake for two hours before catching another hour's sleep. He woke at 5 am and was unable to get back to sleep, getting up as usual at 7 am. On Tuesday night you can see that Sam got up for a period during the night. On Wednesday and Sunday nights it took him several hours to get to sleep. On Sunday night he got up briefly to go to the toilet, and then could not get back to sleep.

Sam usually gets up for work at 7am. We can see that he slept in on Wednesday and was late for work. We can also see that he slept in on Saturday and Sunday. Sam says that

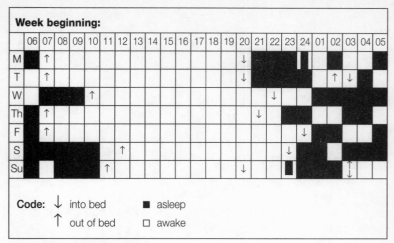

Figure 16.2: Sam's sleep chart

he tends to sleep better on Friday and Saturday nights, but often worries about work on Sunday night. We can see the effect on his sleep pattern.

Sam totalled 46 hours of sleep for the week. He spent about 72 hours in bed, as accurately as can be detected from this chart. This gives Sam a sleep efficiency of 46 out of 72, or 64 per cent.

Keeping a sleep chart like this for a couple of weeks can allow you to identify some patterns, and to calculate your average hours of sleep per night. As a rule, I don't recommend that you keep it for much longer because of the risk that you could become too focused on when you're sleeping and when you're not, and actually compound the problem.

NORMAL SLEEP PATTERNS

Research suggests that, as far as 'normal' can be determined, it is physiologically normal to sleep for between 29 and 33 per cent of the day, or between seven and eight hours. In 2002, Daniel Kripke and colleagues published the results of their analysis of information from more than one million people who were asked in the 1980s about the duration of sleep and frequency of insomnia as part of a study into cancer prevention. Eighty-six per cent of women and 87 per cent of men slept between six and eight hours per night. Fifty-one percent of women and 30 per cent of men reported insomnia at least some nights per month.

Interestingly, many people who complained of insomnia reported sleeping just as many hours as those who did not report insomnia. In other words, the experience of insomnia is somewhat subjective. One person may experience a given number of hours of sleep as unsatisfactory, while another may have no complaint about the same number of hours. This study found that there did not appear to be any long-term risk to life from sleeping for only a short period each night, provided that women averaged at least three-and-a-half hours of sleep and men averaged at least four-and-a-half hours of sleep. In fact, a report of insomnia, whether infrequent or even ten times or more per month, appeared to be associated with a lower risk of dying, as long as it was not associated with the regular use of sleeping pills. (It would not appear to be healthy to use sleeping pills regularly or in the long term, although since the participants in this study were interviewed in the 1980s, some of them may have been taking older sleeping tablets that are no longer in use. There was no evidence to suggest that the occasional use of sleeping pills was harmful.)

In this study, the people with the lowest mortality rate reported sleeping an average of between six-and-a-half and seven-and-a-half hours per night. Of course, these figures are averages and do not tell us what is right for the individual. We don't know what other factors may have contributed to the greater longevity seen in some individuals. However, it does reassure us that insomnia, while unpleasant, is not necessarily harmful, a concern that exacerbates the anxiety of many insomniacs and often sees them lying in bed thinking, 'I've got to get to sleep! I've got to get to sleep! Oh no, I'm not sleepy!' Needless to say, this only increases anxiety and arousal and chases sleep even further away.

Sleep laboratory research, where people are observed and monitored through the night, has also shown that brief awakenings through the night are common and harmless. Most people are not even aware of them, and even after several awakenings can wake feeling refreshed in the morning.

GOALS FOR GOOD SLEEP

Aim to get the number of hours of sleep per night on which you feel your best, but don't be alarmed if you don't manage this every night. In addition, aim for a high sleep efficiency. That is, ideally you want to be sleeping for most of the time you are in bed, and not lying awake. To put it another way, you don't want to waste time lying in bed when you are not sleeping. Sam's sleep efficiency is only 64 per cent. This means that one-third of the time he is in bed is spent lying there awake, an uncomfortable experience.

It is also desirable to be able to fall asleep quickly and, of course, to wake feeling refreshed. Scientists have discovered a number of principles to promote the achievement of good-quality sleep. These principles are often referred to as 'sleep hygiene'.

SLEEP HYGIENE

Perhaps the most important factor in promoting regular sleep is a regular rising time. This is contrary to what most of us would expect. Most people put the emphasis on the time they go to bed, and attempt to compensate for a bad night by going to bed early the next night. You can see in his sleep chart where Sam has attempted this on Monday and Tuesday nights. On Sunday night he went to bed early thinking that it would help him to get a good night's sleep before his return to work on Monday. You can also see that this policy was not particularly successful. He got no more sleep on Monday and Tuesday nights when he also tried going to bed early. On Sunday night it also took him several hours to get to sleep. In fact, this was because he had had so much sleep the night before, sleeping in until eleven o'clock both Saturday and Sunday mornings.

It is now known that the 'body clock' is set by the time of rising, not the time we go to bed. If you calculate that you need seven hours of sleep, then it follows that you will have 17 hours of being awake. You can't really expect to be able to go to sleep again until you have been up for these 17 hours. In Sam's case, on Sunday he was attempting to go to sleep again after he had been awake only nine hours. It was doomed to fail!

If you are experiencing regular insomnia, you really need to aim to *get up at the same time every day*—even on weekends—until the problem is fixed. For most people it is sensible to set this time as being the time you need to get up for work. If you are not working, choose a time that you feel is reasonable. Be sure to make this time realistic. For example, most young adults find it very difficult to get up early unless they really have to. For a young adult who is a student or unemployed, nine o'clock in the morning is probably going to be more realistic than seven o'clock. Do aim to get up in the morning, rather than the afternoon, however, since humans are attuned to daylight and morning light seems particularly beneficial in setting the body clock (and perhaps also in lifting the mood in cases of depression). Once you have set a reasonable and realistic rising time, aim to get up as close to this time as possible every day. To set the body clock most effectively you need to get up *within half an hour* of your set time.

The time you go to bed is less important, although it is desirable to *get to bed around the same time each night*. Going to bed when you start to feel sleepy is usually recommended. This is often referred to as 'catching the sleep wave'. Some people leave it too late. Instead of catching the sleep wave to go to bed, they snuggle down on the sofa and fall asleep in front of the television. They wake uncomfortably some hours later (sofas are not ideal for your posture) and then have trouble falling asleep when they eventually get into bed. At the same time, it's important not to go to bed too early in the evening, or you are likely to spend some time awake. The time you go to bed must be linked to the time you get up, by being a reasonable amount of time later. For example, if you need eight hours sleep and get up at 8 am, then you really don't need to go to bed until 11.30 or so, allowing a little time to fall asleep. On Saturday night, Sam spent 12 hours in bed. There was no way he was going to sleep this long! If you estimate that you need seven hours sleep, and you spend ten hours in bed, then you are almost guaranteeing that you will spend three hours awake at some point during the night—perhaps all at once, possibly with trouble getting to sleep, or perhaps split into several wakeful periods.

If you have a late night occasionally, it doesn't really matter. Remember, you are aiming to get a certain number of hours per night on average. Note that this is not the same as aiming to average a certain number of hours. Let me explain. Let's say that you have decided that eight hours is what you need. Your aim is that *on most nights* you will try to get eight hours of sleep. If you have less sleep on a few nights, this doesn't seem to matter, although certainly the more nights you achieve it, the better rested you will feel. *You do not need to make up for lost sleep.* A myth seems to have arisen that if you have less sleep one night you must make up for it the next night. I have even seen this written in some magazine articles and newspaper features. This theory says that if you need eight hours sleep per night, then you must get 7 x 8 hours sleep per week, or 56 hours. Therefore, if you get only five hours one night because your child kept you awake, you must make up three hours at some other time. This explains why so many people feel they should sleep in on the weekend. There is no evidence that this is the case, and, as we have seen, good evidence that this is simply untrue. It also contributes to the erratic sleep patterns that many people suffer. If you miss out on some sleep one night, it is definitely best to get up at the usual time the next day, and go to bed at the usual time or *slightly* earlier if you are tired then. Do not go to bed earlier simply because you think you should! If you follow these principles, and don't interfere with your body's natural functioning (for example, by worrying too much or going to bed too early), your body will compensate naturally by making your sleep more efficient the night after a night of reduced sleep.

Exercise promotes more restful sleep. It has been shown to promote the deepest stage of sleep, which it is believed may assist in feeling more refreshed the next day. This is yet another reason to make exercise a regular part of your life. The only guideline here is to avoid exercising too close to bedtime. Most experts recommend that you finish exercise two to three hours before retiring for the night. Similarly, it is not recommended to have a heavy meal too close to bedtime.

Caffeine is a stimulant, which is why it is sometimes used to help people stay awake. It continues to exert its effects for many hours. It is recommended that you *avoid caffeine later than mid-afternoon* if you suffer from insomnia. Needless to say, other stimulants should also be avoided close to bedtime.

Sleep is easier and of better quality when your room is *cool, dark and quiet.* (Getting too hot at night is a common cause of nightmares.) Consider investing in window covers that block out light effectively if there are bright lights outside your window or if you are a shift worker and must try to sleep during the day. Noisy environments make it difficult to sleep soundly. However, this does not mean that you have to eliminate all noise. Some noises are easy to accommodate, and may even help to mask more objectionable noises. For example, the 'white noise' of a fan or the static noise a television set makes when there is no programming can help mask the noise of a barking dog (although I don't advise a television set in the bedroom unless you have no trouble sleeping at all). Traffic noise, if it is not too loud, is also a kind a white noise, but honking horns, air brakes and very loud traffic can interfere with sleep. Ticking clocks and dripping taps can be adjusted to, since they are regular and not very loud—but you will need to program yourself to ignore them. If this is not possible, fix the tap and move the clock.

One rule the experts suggest is that we *reserve bed for sleep and sex*. Sex actually promotes good sleep and so is allowed! But it is best that we don't watch television, read, listen to the radio, complete paperwork, worry about the coming day, or argue with our partner. Additionally, we should not allow ourselves to lie awake for hours in bed. This is based on principles of behaviour modification known to psychologists as 'operant conditioning', and was well illustrated by Pavlov's experiments with dogs. Pavlov observed that when dogs were shown a piece of meat they began to salivate in anticipation of eating it. He then began to ring a bell shortly before producing the meat. Soon Pavlov was able to demonstrate that just ringing the bell would cause the dogs to salivate, even without any sign of the meat. The dogs had come to associate the ringing of the bell with the fact that an enticing piece of meat would shortly appear. If you spend long periods in bed lying awake you will unconsciously come to associate being in bed with being awake. Instead of the pleasant anticipation the dogs experienced, yours will be an unpleasant anticipation, since lying in bed at night feeling as though you are the only one in the whole world not sleeping is not to be recommended. Doubly so if you also worry about the negative effects the lack of sleep may have on your ability to function the next day.

Many people are surprised by the recommendation against reading or watching television in bed. They argue that it helps to relax them. I agree that there are many people who have no trouble falling asleep as soon as they put their book down or turn off the television. If these people sleep well through the night and have no complaints about their quality of sleep, then there is no problem. On the other hand, if you are dissatisfied with your sleep pattern, then I strongly recommend that you try implementing the principles of sleep hygiene fairly strictly. Once your sleep is under control, you can try gradually re-introducing some of these other activities if you really miss them.

The principles of operant conditioning also underlie the recommendation about not spending longer than 20 minutes at a time awake in bed. This specific recommendation is also referred to as 'stimulus control'. If you are not asleep in 20 minutes you should get up out of bed. You then engage in some restful activity such as reading, while waiting for another sleep wave. When you feel sleepy you go to bed again. If you are not asleep in 20 minutes, then you get up again. Although this might sound like some kind of torture, it trains you to go to sleep when you go to bed—which is exactly what you want to be able to do. It might only take a few weeks to create better habits.

The need to *control your worry and rumination in bed* has been emphasised in previous chapters. You don't want to associate bed with worry! Techniques for achieving this were discussed with attention focusing on page 161.

It is helpful to prepare yourself for sleep by 'winding down'. Stop working, sit quietly and relax. It is usually suggested that you allow an hour for this if you can, but any time can be helpful. Stop the housework, put away the studies or paperwork, and give your system a chance to quieten down in preparation for sleep.

At this point, it is necessary to mention *sleep rituals*. This is something fairly specific to anxious people, particularly those who have developed a great deal of anxiety about not sleeping. They often have beliefs such as:

- If I don't sleep I won't be able to cope tomorrow.
- If I don't sleep I will be really anxious tomorrow.
- If I don't sleep I will get sick.

I ask people what they mean by 'not coping'. This phrase carries the vague threat of going insane, collapsing, having a nervous breakdown. Is this what happens when people don't get their full quota of sleep? Of course not! How could women ever survive having babies if that were the case? Luckily humans are built a bit more robustly than that. Having no sleep at all for days at a time is demoralising—which is why it has been used as a torture—but it does not kill people or even send them insane. In any case, it is highly unlikely that you are having *no* sleep. The fact of the matter is, you will feel tired, and you may be somewhat less efficient at work and at home, but that's about the worst of it. It's not pleasant, but it's not a catastrophe either. By catastrophising about the results of not sleeping well you will increase your anxiety and arousal level and make it less likely that you will be able to relax and fall asleep.

Some people become so preoccupied with creating what they believe are just the right conditions for sleep that if some little thing is not exactly right, they cannot relax. I have known patients who had elaborate sleep rituals. Firstly, they would go outside and listen for any noise likely to disturb them. Then they would go inside and listen carefully at all the doors and windows. They would then do the rounds of the house checking for any potential sources of noise. Next, they would have specific routines regarding a pre-bedtime drink, night-time bathing, tooth brushing and so forth. Some men were forbidden to come to bed until their female partners were asleep, as the women feared their partner's snoring or even heavy breathing would keep them awake.

There are several problems with trying to set such specific conditions. It is very hard to achieve them, and if you believe that you will sleep only if conditions are ideal, then you are setting yourself up to have problems. Additionally, all that checking is quite anxiety provoking—not the ideal winding-down activity prior to bedtime.

The principles of sleep hygiene

- Regular rising time (essential).
- Regular retiring time (desirable).
- Catch the sleep wave.
- Regular exercise.
- Avoid eating a heavy meal within two hours of retiring.
- Avoid strenuous exercise within two hours of retiring.
- Avoid caffeine from mid-afternoon onwards.
- Make your bedroom cool, dark and quiet.
- Control worry and rumination in bed.
- Bed is for sleep and sex:
  - avoid reading, watching television, listening to the radio
  - do not lie awake in bed for longer than 20 minutes at a time.
- Spend a little time 'winding down' before bed.
- Avoid sleep rituals.

CREATING YOUR OWN SLEEP SCHEDULE

First, decide on how many hours of sleep you think is optimal for you. Next, determine what time you will get up each morning. Now work backwards by the number of hours sleep you need, and add a further 20 to 30 minutes for settling in and falling asleep. This is roughly the time at which you should aim to go to bed. It doesn't matter if you occasionally go to bed later, but do try not to go to bed earlier than this time.

Using Sam as an example, he has decided he does best on seven hours sleep. He would like to get up for work at 6.30 in the morning. Working backwards brings him to 11.30 at night, and allowing half an hour to settle in and fall asleep brings him to eleven o'clock. Thus, Sam should in most cases not go to bed before eleven o'clock each evening. On weekends, until he has resolved his sleep problems, he should continue to get up at 6.30 am.

Troubleshooting

(P) 'No matter how hard I try to get up early, I just sleep through the alarm.'

(R) It is common that people who do not have to get up early in the morning start to sleep in later and later. Although there is not general agreement about this, there is a school of thought that holds that humans naturally have a 25-hour cycle, whereas we have established a 24-hour day. Our natural tendency is thus to sleep a little later each day, and when there is nothing to force us to get up earlier, this is exactly what tends to happen. If you have been getting up at midday, or even later, you are probably not going to bed until at least four o'clock in the morning, if not later. No wonder you find it hard to drag yourself out of bed at seven o'clock. There are a couple of options for tackling this problem. You could try to get up just an hour earlier at a time, and gradually work your way backwards. Alternatively, you can try staying up one whole night and not going to bed the next night until seven to eight hours before you plan to get up.

(P) 'I am going to bed at the right time but I still lie awake for hours.'

(R) It can take time to retrain yourself to sleep soundly. Let us imagine that Sam has this problem. He goes to bed at 11 pm as advised, but is still waking through the night. I would ask Sam to keep another sleep diary for two weeks. I would then ask him to calculate his average hours of sleep. Let us say that Sam calculates that he is sleeping an average of five hours per night. He is not sleeping efficiently. A very effective method for improving sleep efficiency—the ability to spend the time in bed actually sleeping—is to use *sleep restriction*. This means that you restrict your time in bed to the duration of time that you tend to sleep. If you only have five hours in which to get your sleep, it increases the likelihood that you will use every minute of those five hours to actually sleep. Your brain won't have the luxury of picking and choosing the hours it will sleep. This technique is akin to saying to yourself, 'All right. If you're not going to use this time to sleep, then I'll take it away from you.' Because you will be somewhat sleep deprived, your body will naturally compensate by trying to sleep more. In this way you will train yourself to sleep more soundly for five hours at a time.

The next step is to train yourself to sleep a little longer. If you feel you need seven hours, your goal is to sleep seven *consecutive* hours, rather than a few hours here and there, separated by periods of wakefulness. For this reason, you extend your time in bed quite gradually, just by half an hour at a time. When you can sleep the full five hours consistently, start going to bed half an hour earlier. When you can sleep five-and-a-half hours consistently (that is, for several nights in a row), go to bed half an hour earlier again. You are now aiming to sleep six consecutive hours. When you can do this consistently, go to bed half an hour earlier. This technique may sound rather draconian, but it is extremely effective and well worth a try.

THE ROLE OF SLEEPING TABLETS

Most doctors are not keen on prescribing sleeping tablets and most people know that they can be habit forming. This means that you reach a point where you cannot sleep without them. Generally, a person will become dependent on sleeping tablets if they take them every night for two weeks or more. Many sleeping tablets also interact with alcohol, and some can have 'hangover-like' effects the next day, impairing alertness and reaction time.

It is important to know that you may experience what is known as 'rebound insomnia' if you try to stop taking sleeping tablets. This can occur when a person who has become dependent on them to sleep, suddenly stops taking them. They may find that they cannot sleep at all for a few nights. In other words, they temporarily get even worse insomnia than they had before they started taking the tablets. While the problem will resolve itself in a few days to a week, many people unfortunately find the experience so unnerving and unpleasant that they go straight back on to the sleeping tablets and may not try again to stop them.

So, given all the negatives, do sleeping tablets have any role at all in treating insomnia? No doubt, if you ask ten different doctors this question, you will get ten different opinions! I will give you my opinion on this, and I stress that it is *my* opinion. You and your doctor should talk over your particulars to determine what is best for you. In my practice I try to avoid having a person take sleeping tablets every night. However, I do sometimes prescribe them for people to take in a controlled and limited way. A typical example would be the person who comes to see me with a long history of poor sleep, who is very tired, and frustrated and demoralised by their inability to sleep. You do need energy and a positive outlook to work at improving your sleep—as you can see from above, many of the strategies take a good deal of will power! So with a person in this state, I would start work on improving their sleep using the strategies above, but have sleeping tablets as a back-up. The rule of thumb I use is that if a person has two or three nights where they get little sleep, then for the next two nights they will take a sleeping tablet an hour or so before going to bed. Note that I do not advise them to take a tablet if they find themselves wide awake in the early hours of the morning. I encourage the use of sleeping tablets in a planned, controlled way; whether a sleeping tablet will be taken is planned in advance, and it is always taken *before* going to bed.

By using sleeping tablets only a few times a week at the most, a person will not become dependent. By not taking them every night, the body will have a chance to develop its own better sleep habits, and the individual will learn not to catastrophise about a poor night's sleep here and there. Yet by having them as a back-up after several night's poor sleep, the individual will still get some relief. Knowing they are available as a back-up, also helps the person to tolerate the bad nights. As the sleep pattern improves, the use of sleeping tablets is gradually phased out.

By following the above principles, even people with a lifetime of poor sleep have at least improved their night's rest, and many people with a shorter or milder history of insomnia have learned to sleep well.

Chapter Seventeen

CONTINUING YOUR OWN PERSONAL PROGRAM

By now you will have a good idea of your own pattern of worry, and will hopefully have tried implementing some of the strategies described. Until these strategies become second nature, you will need to put some effort into continuing to practise them.

THE TIMEFRAME OF IMPROVEMENT

Usually, you will experience improvement in your anxiety level within a few weeks, though it will require considerable effort. After a few months less effort will be required, but you will still experience bouts of worry and have to work at implementing your strategies. It takes about six months before you don't have to think so actively about applying your anxiety management strategies and are using them more habitually.

In the early weeks you will still have worry episodes. The first change you notice may be the ability to terminate these episodes sooner than you could before. In fact, before treatment most people find that the episodes of worry just have to burn themselves out or get supplanted by a new worry. So give yourself a pat on the back if you start to be able to stop a worry episode after a day or two, when it used to go on for a week. With time, you will be able to control it even more quickly, until eventually you can actually prevent excessive worry in response to uncertainty.

It is almost inevitable that you will experience a recurrence of anxiety during this six-month period. Some worry will occur that you haven't met before, or a worry will return that you thought you'd dealt with. Everyone seems to have this experience. Don't lose your nerve! The strategies will work for you again. By overcoming these 'hiccups' your ability to manage your anxiety will get even stronger.

HAS YOUR WORRY IMPROVED?

Do you feel better? You may be able to answer this quite easily. You can also repeat the Penn State Worry Questionnaire at intervals to provide a more objective measure of your improvement, or repeat your worry diary at any time. Often friends and family will notice the difference, too. But what if you do not feel you have improved as much as you hoped? You can go through the checklist of strategies that appears below. You might also consider going to see a GP, psychologist or psychiatrist with expertise in the treatment of anxiety. It can be valuable to have the perspective of someone who is both objective and professionally trained. They may be able to make useful suggestions to help you overcome sticking points, or identify unhelpful behaviours or cognitions that you weren't aware of.

FORMULATING YOUR OWN WORRY MANAGEMENT PROGRAM

Your first step is to make yourself a problem list, as was shown for Rosita in chapter thirteen, and for Jenny in chapter fourteen. Record this in your workbook, along with strategies that might be helpful. Below, I have divided the strategies discussed in this book into the different symptom areas of anxiety to help you to choose appropriate strategies for your symptoms. It may help you to look at each problem and categorise it as being physical, psychological (cognitive) or behavioural. You can also make particular note of the strategies that you have so far identified as being helpful and appropriate in managing your own worry and anxiety.

Physiological (de-arousal) strategies

Implementing these strategies is often the first step in taking control of your worry:

- exercise
- progressive muscular relaxation
- meditation
- better sleep
- other: yoga, tai chi.

Psychological (cognitive) strategies

Through the cognitive challenging exercises you have been asked to create summaries of your challenges. Many people find that the same themes come up for them repeatedly, and they can develop something like a mantra that they can say to themselves as a reminder of the principal worry issue they need to overcome. These themes may include some of the 'cognitive errors' and patterns of thinking that were described earlier:

- catastrophising
- jumping to conclusions
- focusing on the negative
- magical thinking
- treating a possibility like a probability.

You may find it helpful to remind yourself of the sayings:

- When you hear hoof beats, think of horses not zebras.
- Wait and see.

Some of the statements that other people have shared with me over the years, include:

- I've done it before and I can do it again.
- It's not the end of the world.
- One step at a time.

Hopefully, you have also developed some of your own helpful statements by now. You can write these here to remind you:

_____

_____

_____

_____

_____

_____

_____

_____

_____

The Worry Control Blueprint provides a framework for analysing and dealing with worry. Its steps include:

1. Cognitive challenging
- Are your worries realistic?
- Have you overestimated the likelihood of a bad outcome?
- Have you overestimated how bad it would be if the feared outcome occurred?

By completing a number of Worry Control Blueprints for yourself, you may be able to identify a particular pattern. For example, do you always tend to overestimate the likelihood of a disastrous outcome? If so, be alert to this tendency and suspect this faulty pattern of thinking whenever you are worrying. Ask yourself, 'Am I overestimating the likelihood of something bad happening?' This can help you deal with the anxiety and worry more quickly. If you often tend to have unrealistic worries, you can say to yourself, 'Is this a realistic anxiety?' If you can recognise it as unrealistic you can go straight to the 'Then stop worrying about it!' step. Many people tend to worry about things they can do nothing about—regrets about things they have done or not done in the past, or events or situations that are simply out of their control. If you tend to have this pattern of worry, you can be alert for it, and say at an early stage, 'Well, there's nothing I can do about it.' Then stop thinking about it!

If your worry is realistic, then the next step is:

2. Structured problem solving
- Can something be done to reduce the likelihood or impact of the feared outcome?
- Get more information if you need it.

Then move on to the final step:

3. Then stop worrying about it!
- Refocus your attention on the task at hand.

Other helpful cognitive strategies include:

- Focus on the most likely outcome.
- Avoid misinterpreting the presence of anxiety as evidence that something must be wrong.
- Avoid misinterpreting the symptoms of anxiety as being symptoms of an illness you fear.
- Confront and learn to live with uncertainty.

Behavioural strategies

Your program will also need to address your anxious behaviours. You will need to:

- Reduce hypervigilance.
- Avoid excessive monitoring of your environment.
- Avoid excessive monitoring of your own body.
- Resist the urge to seek reassurance
  - by checking your work, your body or your environment
  - by asking others whether everything is okay
  - by visiting your doctor excessively or asking for unnecessary tests.
- Confront situations you have been avoiding.
- Make decisions.
- Take responsibility.
- Make commitments.
- Face situations that trigger your anxiety.

Your problem list:

Problem	Strategies
_____	_____
_____	_____
_____	_____
_____	_____
_____	_____
_____	_____
_____	_____
_____	_____
_____	_____

COPING WITH RECURRENCES

It's unlikely that you'll never be anxious again. However, if you catch your symptoms early, you can prevent a full-blown anxiety state from developing. Your physical, cognitive and behavioural strategies will work for you. As a general guideline, *go back to basics*. That is, start from the beginning and go through all the strategies you used before in a structured way. When you do this, it is almost certain that those strategies will work for you once again. Although relapses are unpleasant, with continued practice of your anxiety management skills they will become less frequent and less severe.

By consistently employing all the strategies in your personal program you can look forward to a life free of excessive worry and unreasonable anxiety.

Bibliography

Andrews G, Hall W, Teesson M, Henderson S. 1999, *The Mental Health of Australians*, Mental Health Branch, Commonwealth Department of Health and Aged Care.

Nelson, Craig. 2000, *Let's Get Lost*, Headline Book Publishing, London, p 286.

Ost, L-G. 1987, 'Applied relaxation: description of a coping technique and review of controlled studies', *Behaviour Research and Therapy*, vol. 25, pp. 397–409.

Diagnostic and Statistical Manual of Mental Disorders, 1994, 4th edn, American Psychiatric Association, Washington DC, p. 395.

MIMS Annual, 2003, June, MediMedia Australia, St Leonards, NSW, pp. 3–328.

Index

obsessive compulsive
disorder (OCD), 1, 13,
15–17, 58
magical thinking, 79
treatment, 16
operant conditioning,
233–234

pain, 7, 18, 58
panic attacks, 1, 12, 13,
18–19, 58
hyperventilation, 65
paraesthesias, 18
Penn State Worry
Questionnaire, 41–42,
114, 242
perfectionism, 144–151
personalising, 150
physiological strategies,
243
placebo effect, 46–48
plane travel, fear of, 21
positive thinking, 80–81
post-traumatic stress
disorder (PTSD), 13,
17–18
verbal versus visual, 81
probability overestimation,
84–86, 139–140,
142–144, 166,
199–200, 243
problem solving
identification of
problem, 101–102,
149
strategies, 51, 52

structured *see* structured
problem solving
procrastination, 1, 39–40
professional help, 54–57
psychiatry, 55–56
psychology, 55–56
psychological strategies,
243–245
psychosis, 92
public speaking, 21

reaction
choosing the form of,
148, 165–166, 207
reassurance-seeking, 58,
185–186, 211–212
appropriate, 194–198
graded exposure
program, 221–222
resisting, 167–168, 170,
194–198, 207,
212–215
relaxation, 1, 14, 51, 52,
197–198, 243
practice record, 68–69
progressive muscular,
52, 62–64, 163–164,
174
queries and tips, 67
sleep and, 52–53, 224,
234–236
risk assessment, 87–88
just do it!, 176
structured problem
solving, 110–111
rumination, 75–76

support groups, 56
sweating, 7, 18, 20, 58
symptoms, 7
    behavioural, 58
    GAD, 26–27
    physiological, 58
    psychological, 58

tai chi, 67, 243
teenagers, 4
tension, 1
thought
    cognitive challenging *see*
        cognitive challenging
    emotions and, 125–127
    identifying, 124–129
    realistic thinking,
        129–134
tranquillisers, 28
trembling, 7, 18, 20, 58

uncertainty, fear of, 7, 27,
    30, 37, 39–40, 245
    what-if-itis, 74–75, 93

Valium, 28
vomiting, 7, 21, 58

wait and see strategy,
    166–167, 169, 172,
    206–207

walking, 60–61
what-if-itis *see* uncertainty,
    fear of
work life
    impact of worry on, 1
worry *see also* anxiety
    anxiety reduction, 82–83
    benefits, 76–83
    characteristics, 75–76
    control blueprint *see*
        control
    management program,
        242–243
    patterns, personal, 73
    record, 70–73
    verbal versus visual, 81
Worry Control Blueprint,
        93, 96–99, 156,
        158–159, 168–169,
        203, 208
    physiological strategies,
        243
    psychological strategies,
        243–245

Xanax, 28

yoga, 61, 67–68, 243